WBI LEARNING RESOURCES SERIES

Cities in a Globalizing World

Governance, Performance, and Sustainability

Edited by
Frannie Léautier

The World Bank
Washington, DC

ISBN: 0-8213-6553-3
E-ISBN: 0-8213-6554-1
13-digit ISBN (EAN): 978-0-8213-6553-3
13-digit E-ISBN: 978-0-8213-6554-0
DOI: 10.1596/ 978-0-8213-6553-3

Chapter 2, "Globalization and Urban Infrastructure," is adapted from *Perspectives on Globalization of Infrastructure,* by Frannie Léautier and Andrew C. Lemer, published in 2003 as a World Bank Institute Working Paper (Washington, DC: World Bank).

Chapter 3, "Globalization and Urban Performance," is adapted from *Governance and the City,* by Daniel Kaufmann, Frannie Léautier, and Massimo Mastruzzi, published in 2005 as Policy Research Working Paper 3712 (Washington, DC: World Bank).

Library of Congress Cataloging-in-Publication Data

Cities in a globalizing world : governance, performance and sustainability / edited by Frannie Léautier.
    p. cm.—(WBI learning resources series)
  Includes bibliographical references and index.
  ISBN-13: 978-0-8213-6553-3
  ISBN-10: 0-8213-6553-3
  ISBN-13: 978-0-8213-6554-0 (e-book)
  ISBN-10: 0-8213-6554-1 (e-book)
  1. Urban policy. 2. Urban poor. 3. Municipal government. 4. Municipal services. 5. Sustainable development. 6. Globalization. I. Léautier, Frannie. II. World Bank. III. Series.

HT151.C5686 2006
307.76—dc22

2005057897

Contents

Figures

Tables

Annexes

Contributors

Séverine Dinghem is a senior financial officer in the Infrastructure, Economics, and Finance Group of the World Bank.

Daniel Kaufmann is director of the Global Programs Group of the World Bank Institute.

Frannie Léautier is vice president of the World Bank Institute.

Andrew C. Lemer is president of the MATRIX Group, LLC, in Baltimore, Maryland.

Massimo Mastruzzi is a research analyst in the Global Programs Group of the World Bank Institute.

Barjor Mehta is a senior urban specialist in the Infrastructure, Finance, and Private Sector Department of the World Bank Institute.

Acknowledgments

Many of the ideas that shaped this book were born out of a series of conversations I had over a period of two years with Nick Stern when he was Chief Economist at the World Bank. I thank him for his many insights and suggestions. Francois Bourguignon, the Bank's Chief Economist, provided valuable comments throughout the writing process.

I would like to thank all those who provided substantive and editorial advice on various chapters, especially Tim Campbell and Christine Kessides at the World Bank, Nemat Shafik when she was World Bank Vice President for Infrastructure, Remy Prud'homme at the University of Paris in Creteil, Nic Retsinas at the Joint Center on Housing at Harvard University, Richard Stren at Toronto University, and the participants who attended a presentation we made on "Governance and the City: An Empirical Exploration into Global Determinants of Urban Performance," at the Annual Bank Conference on Development Economics (ABCDE) in Brussels in 2004.

I am also grateful to my coauthors who agreed to help me explore some exciting new frontiers in urban management and governance, and to my colleagues in WBI who, in many different ways, supported and contributed to the publication of this work.

Frannie A. Léautier, Vice President
The World Bank Institute

Foreword

World Bank research shows that in 2003, 48 percent of the world's population (3 billion people) lived in urban areas—a 33 percent increase from the 1990 level. By 2020, 4.1 billion people (55 percent of the world's population) will live in urban areas. Almost 94 percent of the increase will occur in developing countries. By 2015, there will be 22 megacities (cities or agglomeration with a population of more than 8 million) and 475 cities with populations exceeding 1 million. The forces of urbanization promise to reshape the developing world, presenting both opportunities and challenges across the socioeconomic spectrum.

At the same time, globalization is becoming the driving force behind economic growth and development. Cities will have to compete for foot-loose investment flows to generate jobs for their growing urban labor force; and they will have to provide security and access to services and urban infrastructure for their growing urban populations. This will present enormous challenges for local governments, requiring substantial improvement in local capacity and performance. The extent to which individual cities can respond to these challenges depends on a mix of factors—some that are outside any city's immediate control, some within its control—such as individual city policies and local governance.

Cities in a Globalizing World sheds new light on the dynamics and associations among globalization, urbanization, and local governance. It demonstrates how close these associations are and how crucial they will increasingly become for sustainable development. It also makes clear that better policy design in the field of urbanization will depend on improved analysis of causality, which in turn will require the collection of much better quality data. This book will be of great interest to students and practitioners of urban management and those concerned with globalization and the developing world.

François J. Bourguignon
Senior Vice President & Chief Economist,
Development Economics, The World Bank

Introduction

For centuries the rural poor have seen cities as places where they can find new opportunities, with the promise of a better life. For city residents, the rural areas have been seen as critical for providing fresh food, a clean and undisturbed environment to travel to and where they can rest, and for many generations, until recently, a place that most city residents called "home." Whatever the relationship may have been between perception and reality in the past, there is no doubt that the reality is being transformed. The pace of urbanization in the last 40 years has grown tremendously and people have not only been moving from the rural areas to cities, but from town to city, city to city, and from one country to another.

Within a generation, most of the developing world's population will live in urban areas; and the number of urban residents will double. As a result of this massive migration to cities urban poverty has actually grown faster than rural poverty, and some cities have not been able to deliver the promise of a better life for their new migrants. Looking forward, the infrastructure that will be built (or not) in the next 20 years will shape the patterns and functioning of the cities and the lives of their inhabitants for generations to come.

Urban poverty is multidimensional. It includes limited access to employment opportunities and income, inadequate and insecure housing and services, violent and unhealthy environments, few or no social protection mechanisms, and limited access to adequate health and education opportunities. This poverty is generally marked by deplorable living conditions; inadequate sanitation, air pollution, crime, and many other conditions that contribute to ill health and a fragile existence. Environmental degradation in cities has particularly severe impacts on poor urban residents. And there are also serious national and global consequences.

Africa has experienced the most rapid urbanization the world has ever seen. Some 37 percent of Africans now live in cities and that figure will rise to more than 50 percent over the next 20 years. Currently over 150 million people live in slums without municipal services; and local authorities in Africa lack the appropriate resources and capacities to manage the rapid urbanization process. The Report of the Commission for Africa, for which I directed the writing, argued strongly that any strategy for growth and poverty reduction must place urbanization centre stage.

The World Bank recognizes the growing importance of cities and the responsibility of local governments for delivering many of the services that have direct impact on people's daily lives. Well-functioning urban systems that include the communities themselves and that partner with national government are critical to the lives of urban residents, current and future, and to economic growth: only by managing the social, economic, and environmental transitions to an urban world can cities and towns become sustainable, fulfill the promise of development for their inhabitants, and contribute to the progress of the country as a whole—especially in an expanding global economy.

As an engine of economic growth, globalization can be a major force for poverty reduction especially in urban areas. But many of the developing countries, particularly in Africa, do not have the appropriate policy foundations, economic base, or managerial capacities to promote the good governance and policy that can realize the full benefits from the trade, investments, and financial flows that globalization promotes. Potential investors, both national and foreign, assess carefully the quality of life and access to critical infrastructural and services in a given city before taking their decisions.

Cities in a Globalizing World contributes to the empirical and theoretical analysis of the performance of cities in a globalizing world, bringing together a range of perspectives on the policy implications for urban management. It provides guidance for policymakers on ways of capitalizing on the global economy that will make the most of the cities resources and managerial infrastructure as well as guiding investment and policy for the future. The book provides examples of how conflicts can be managed between individual and collective interests, such as the extensive environmental and social consultation undertaken in the planning and implementation of the Jamuna Bridge in Bangladesh, which now joins cities that had never seen daily connection between people in markets. The authors present empirical evidence that suggests that good governance and globalization tend to improve city-level performance in both the access to services as well as the quality of delivery of services which allows cities to translate global opportunity into local value for their citizens. This research also raises difficult questions of causality: does more globalization cause better governance, or vice versa?

The authors look particularly at African cities to examine similarities with and differences from cities elsewhere. Their research suggests that Africa faces the challenge of improving both the quality of the management of its cities and their governance, so that they can offer services that will attract foreign investment while continuing to serve the needs of their residents and their regional economies.

In a world moving very rapidly on both urbanization and globalization, cities in the developing world face both serious challenges and attractive opportunities. They can reap the benefits of economic growth by creating an enabling investment climate: well-functioning markets, institutions that support sound governance and regulatory regimes, and public infrastructure and social services. At the same time they can create an environment where their citizens are both included and empowered. And because cities do not exist in isolation, urban policies and programs must also be coordinated with national initiatives. *Cities in a Globalizing World* not only raises our awareness of issues that can only become still more pressing and still more critical to growth and equity in this century; it also provides important and valuable analyses of options for public action.

Sir Nicholas Stern
Head of Government Economic Service
United Kingdom

1

Understanding Cities in a Globalizing World

Frannie Léautier

Although globalization has been going on for centuries, as human settlements have grown and become interconnected by transportation, migration, and trade routes, globalization has picked up speed remarkably in the past few decades. Globalization's twin engines of opportunity and competition have transformed businesses and workers everywhere, and increasingly they are transforming the cities where those businesses and workers reside. Cities have always been the first ports of call for outsiders, sometimes the key prizes of conquest, and from their inception the sites of interaction among peoples, whether on trade, culture, or diplomacy. Cities today find themselves in a global space where they are asked to compete with each other—even without desiring to do so—and many times without the traditional support they have enjoyed from their national governments. What makes some cities prosper in this new environment, while others seem to stagnate? How do the pressures of globalization affect the quality of life in a city? Some hypotheses suggest that strong cities grow stronger, while weak cities seem to get weaker—unless they undertake corrective actions. These must be actions designed to propel the weaker cities into the ranks of cities considered to have good business addresses or to be great places to visit or reside. City managers and urban policy makers respond to these hypotheses, which are many times founded on weak empirical evidence. They seem to assume that global businesses favor cities with strong performance in matters such as infrastructure services, quality of life indicators, and human resources.

In this book, we bring together empirical and theoretical analyses of the performance of cities in a globalizing world. Several of the chapters use an empirical approach to examine whether the influx of global business, including connections with international markets, tends on balance to improve or degrade existing city infrastructure, services, and governance. Other chapters use game theory to model the interactions of the citizens, firms, and mayor in a city or look at the historical development of cities to assess the impact of technology and scale. Each of the studies presented here seeks to understand the connections among urbanization, globalization, and governance, often by examining cases where those forces are joined most successfully, but also by considering cases where they diverge, as they do in many African cities.

Each chapter brings a different perspective to the question of how globalization is affecting cities, but all consider the policy implications of their findings and propose directions for future research. Together, they are intended to guide city managers and national policy makers intent on seeking economic growth in the global economy or improving the quality of life for their citizens by showing what specific interventions—enhancing services and human resources, for example—are most likely to attract the kind of global activities, such as finance, trade, and tourism, that will complement rather than tax their cities' existing strengths.

Globalization and Urbanization Infrastructure

In Chapter 2, Frannie Léautier and Andrew C. Lemer argue that the main challenge facing infrastructure professionals today is embodied in the precept, "Think globally, act locally." Although the facilities and services of infrastructure are still seen by public works managers and users as essentially local, the underlying demands for infrastructure and the means employed in its finance and development are increasingly global in scope. Business relationships and production often cross national boundaries and time zones. Most important, for increasing numbers of those who concern themselves with infrastructure development and management, the ways of thinking about infrastructure and making decisions are undergoing fundamental changes.

Infrastructure itself has become an export industry, creating pockets of wealth held by the firms and employees who own and operate the infrastructure on which a widely dispersed and sometimes resentful consumer base relies for transport services, drinking water, energy, and waste disposal. Local communities have shown increasing resistance to the presence of infrastructure facilities, even if those facilities could provide substantially improved services to the community. Because infrastructure draws on financial markets that have become global in scope, what might once have been local liquidity problems spill over into international affairs. Financial upheavals in Mexico in the 1980s, Asia in the late 1990s, and Turkey and Argentina a decade later have forced development economists to rethink the once-promising role of private financing in infrastructure development and management. The September 11, 2001, terrorist attack on the United States and the multiple attacks on the transport system in London in July 2005 have invigorated and added international dimensions to discussions of local vulnerability and security. How are we to resolve the inherent—and seemingly inevitable—conflict between accommodating individual interests and serving collective preferences, between meeting immediate demands and providing for future generations, or between maintenance for daily use and maintenance for more security?

The resolution is achievable, if at all, only at the level of individual projects and enterprises. The chapter explores five specific cases in which local infrastructure projects had broad implications for governance and economic development in their regions: The protection of parkland in the path of a planned interstate highway in Memphis, Tennessee, USA; the extensive environmental and social consultation in planning the Chad-Cameroon Petroleum and Pipeline Development Project; the multiparty institutional arrangements devised in constructing the Jamuna Bridge in Bangladesh; the broad environmental impacts and local jurisdictional interests balanced in the Deer Island Waste Treatment Facility Project in Boston, Massachusetts, USA; and the technological innovation and institutional reforms in support of small-scale enterprises employed in a distributed energy project in Uganda.

Examples such as these illustrate four broad dimensions of change characterizing the evolution of globalized infrastructure, an evolution toward more effectively resolving conflicts between individual and collective interests and between people's immediate demands and society's desire to provide for future generations.

- *Democratization.* When the environmentally minded citizens of Memphis and the villagers and farmers along the Jamuna River became a part of the decision making that shaped a major infrastructure investment, they exemplified a trend toward more democratic participation in the decision-making process. Clever use of the political process, requirements imposed by delay-averse financiers, and pressures of world opinion have motivated inclusion of a wider range of "stakeholder" interests in infrastructure investment and operations.
- *Decentralization.* The emergence of small-scale producers and a distributed supply system in Uganda's power sector illustrates a general trend in infrastructure management toward less centralized control and smaller-scale production processes enabled by new technologies. The immense success of the automobile reflects an early instance of the trend now most apparent in energy supply and telecommunications.
- *Diffusion.* The rise of multinational infrastructure providers prepared to plan, build, and operate infrastructure in other countries represents a major shift from the historical unwillingness of investors to lend money across borders. In addition, the development of cadres of professionals in many places, educated at a relatively few world-class institutions, has both facilitated the spread of ideas and provided the intellectual resources needed to adapt those ideas to the specific conditions of site and situation. Ideas are now transported across countries by rising numbers of migrants, through their use of modern communications tools, but also through their financial contribution to their home countries by way of remittances. Remittances allow people who have left their home countries to still contribute to the local economy, bringing ideas on how those monies can be spent.
- *Diversification.* The expansion of the range of services expected of infrastructure has been motivated by the increased difficulty of putting new infrastructure into service. This difficulty reflects not only the greater number of voices involved in decision making, but also the higher priority now given to protection of wildlife habitat and social stability of communities, for example, than might have been the case several decades ago. The concept of the "capital" invested in infrastructure is now recognizing that pristine streams, close-knit neighborhoods, and historic structures have resource value that may not be fully reflected in current market prices.

The authors foresee a growing need for institutions that can facilitate collective action in infrastructure development and management. Such institutions will supplement traditional government agencies, elected officials, and infrastructure professionals by enhancing decision makers' sensitivity to the indicators of local communities' concerns, including communities at the fringe, and facilitating the balancing of different groups' interests, including those of future generations, and executing and implementing agreed decisions with commitment and accountability to all key stakeholders.

Globalization and Urban Performance

Following the discussion of urban infrastructure is an exploration of the impact of globalization on urban performance (Chapter 3). Daniel Kaufmann, Frannie Léautier, and Massimo Mastruzzi construct a preliminary worldwide database for more than 400 cities, containing indicators of globalization at the country and city level, as well as variables on city governance, city performance (such as access and quality of infrastructure service delivery), and other relevant city characteristics. They begin by defining urban governance, following UNESCO, as the processes that steer and take into account the links among stakeholders, local authorities, and citizens to favor active participation and negotiation among actors, transparent decision-making mechanisms, and innovation in urban management policies. They regard urban governance and globalization as outcomes that are visible to citizens of the city, which allows empirical tests of the city as a "place" or as an "enduring performance." The authors explore the key determinants of city performance using a simple conceptual framework and a set of hypotheses, and then test them econometrically using existing data and new data gathered in their research.

Based on empirical evidence, they find that good governance and globalization tend to improve city-level performance on both the access to infrastructure services and the quality of delivery. Furthermore, their results show complex interactions among technology, governance, and city performance, as well as evidence of a non-linear (∪-shaped) relationship between city size and performance, challenging the view that very large cities necessarily exhibit lower performance and pointing to potential agglomeration economies. Port cities seem to be in general more dependent on good governance for the city performance variables that matter for globalization (access to cell phone, internet access), and capital cities tend more to serve local interests, as seen, for instance, in better access to local services (water sewerage, electricity) in such cities. These results are explored further in Chapter 6.

Although the authors find that globalization and governance are positively correlated with each other at the city level, the simple conceptual and econometric model used in this chapter could not resolve the direction of causality: Does more globalization cause better governance, or vice versa? The simple model is extended in subsequent chapters in this volume and could be augmented by further research with additional data and a more complex econometric model.

Nonetheless, even in the simple model, the evidence suggests the importance of focusing policy reforms on improving countrywide governance, thereby tapping into economic benefits for the country at large but also providing a platform for cities to benefit from such national improvements. The evidence also suggests that improving governance at the city level allows cities to translate global opportunity into local value for their citizens. This implies that reformist city leaders do have important local policy and institutional levers at their disposal: Governance at the local level matters significantly for urban performance. Finally, it is important to work with cities to support their globalization process and status by, for example, encouraging cities to place procurement and budget information on the city website and to network with other cities to tap into global opportunities.

Urban Performance Profiles:
The Impact of Globalization and the Challenge for Africa

Drawing on work presented in Chapters 3 and 5, Frannie Léautier and Barjor Mehta use two sets of empirical explorations to examine whether the influx of global business, including connections with international markets, tends on balance to improve or degrade existing city performance. In Chapter 4, they first compare city performance profiles on a number of dimensions, asking whether globalization does indeed seem to favor well-performing cities. Second, they look at the specific case of Africa to see if urban dynamics there are the same or different in comparison with cities elsewhere.

When companies or citizens choose a city in which to locate, they pay attention to issues such as the quality of life and access to critical infrastructural and social services. Observed city performance profiles, therefore, exhibit mutual interdependence between the attained level of globalization and the performance of the city—unless city managers are not responsive to signals from firms or citizens. Such a case would occur if cities are badly governed, or if the levers that city managers can use are few.

Léautier and Mehta use an index of country-level globalization developed by A. T. Kearney and *Foreign Policy* Magazine, which assesses changes in the components of globalization measured by:

- *Political engagement:* The number of memberships in international organizations, UN Security Council missions in which each country participates, and foreign embassies that each country hosts.
- *Technology:* The number of internet users, internet hosts, and secure servers.
- *Personal contact:* International travel and tourism, international telephone traffic, and cross-border transfers.
- *Economic integration:* Trade, foreign direct investment and portfolio capital flows, and income payments and receipts.

The authors find that in more-globalized countries cities grow at a slower pace than in less-globalized countries. Such a trend lends credence to the argument that if a city cannot act as a global player, it needs to rely more on its regional role—serving its hinterland—and hence needs to grow faster to meet the demands of a regional economy. Cities are the main engines of growth for the rural hinterland in less-globalized countries, key regional players in moderately globalized countries, and brokers of local and global interests in highly globalized countries. There are transition costs, as countries move toward more globalization, because cities are sometimes not able to manage the balance between the demand for globally needed services, such as transportation, and locally needed services, such as health, education, and social safety nets.

The city profiles also show that cities in countries that are beginning to globalize provide more employment than those in more-globalized countries, but initially most of the opportunities are informal. Informal activities get absorbed into the formal economy as cities globalize further. Nonetheless, as the pressures of globalization continue to increase, many highly globalized cities once again need an informal economy, even though the long-term pattern is to reduce the dependence on informality. This result, the authors argue, could explain why countries that have poor business environments and hence cannot support new company formation and small-scale enterprises in the formal sector do have these entities in the informal sector. The informal sector in turn becomes a dynamic engine of growth that first taps into global opportunities. The garment industry in Bangladesh is a good example of this phenomenon, as is the leather industry in Africa. Furthermore, the results indicate that how cities are managed broadly affects the differential performance of their economies, over and above the opportunities they may have as a result of globalization.

These results point to three main conclusions for Africa. First, Africa should continue to improve the quality of its decentralization efforts, seeking nuanced solutions, with a smart combination of economic and political factors. Second, the benefits of urbanization in Africa can be tapped only if the larger cities, especially coastal areas, play more of a global or regional role than a local one. Third, there is a need to improve the quality of the management of cities in Africa, so that they can best balance the tension between offering services that make them attractive to foreign investment and continuing to serve the needs of their residents and their regional economies. The need for African cities to be better governed is also acute because good governance in a globalizing world is a key enabler of successful performance of cities, as shown in Chapter 3.

Explaining Urban Performance: Globalization and Governance

Chapter 5 by Frannie Léautier and Séverine Dinghem seeks to understand differences in urban performance by looking at the interactions among citizens, an elected mayor or municipal leader, and a globally oriented firm making the decision to locate in the city. The authors use game theory to show that the dynamics of interactions among citizens, mayors, and firms, within a context of globalization, can improve the performance of cities. This framework attempts to derive the nature of causality from globalization to good governance and from local accountability to good governance. In fact, the analysis shows that both globalization and local accountability matter, but that the interaction between globalization and good governance should lead to better performance than local accountability by itself or globalization in the absence of local accountability. The analysis also shows that, when firms try to influence city leaders and go unchecked, city performance is likely to suffer.

Empirical examples, drawn from the French experience with water contracts, illustrate the outcome of the dynamic simulation. These examples reveal the rather seamy side to globalization, which co-exists with the benefits of globalization. The intensification of the exchanges and increased demands of citizens for good governance also comes with more sophisticated and "hidden" opportunities for bad governance. Typically, financial crimes and money laundering on an international scale make it more and more complex to dismantle embezzlement and corruption in countries that are already exposed to bad governance and lack of transparency. In other words, globalization can amplify good or bad governance. Cities and regions with good governance thus tend to become even more efficient, while cities that are suffering from bad governance tend to become even worse, especially in most African cities and in the old industrial centers in Europe and Central Asia, where it is difficult for the citizens to "exit" from the grip of local authorities.

The authors also stress the importance of information sharing, especially through the powerful global channel of the World Wide Web. What firms and citizens know matters for good governance. Thus, making a range of critical information publicly available, for example, on a city website, improves the possibility of good governance and can lead to better quality of life for the city's citizens. Better information provides better means to control public accountability, and cities can do a lot using web technology to improve the access to information.

The results also indicate that history matters for good governance. A methodology that captures the dynamic interactions among citizens, municipal authorities, and firms over time can shed light on some of the difficult issues surrounding urban governance. Such analysis would be relevant to understand the high urbanization rates in Africa, which have come with little increased welfare for cities, limited economic growth for countries, scarce foreign direct investment for firms, and well-known challenges for governance. Chapter 4 explores these challenges further. Additional research on African cities, using a historical methodology, could also shed light on this difficult topic.

Explaining Urban Performance: Globalization, Technology, and Scale

In the closing chapter, Daniel Kaufmann, Frannie Léautier, and Massimo Mastruzzi investigate the role that various city-level characteristics play in distinguishing the performance of cities as they face the twin pressures for improved local governance driven by the preferences of their citizens and the need for heightened service provision driven by the firms seeking to locate on a global scale. The analysis uses the authors' worldwide database for more than 400 cities, which is also the source for the data in Chapter 3. The evidence suggests that there are particular and complex interactions among the technology choices that citizens and firms have, the quality of local governance, and the overall performance of the city. In particular, the authors confirm the conclusion drawn in Chapter 3 that port cities seem to be more dependent than nonports on good governance for the city performance variables that matter for globalization (access to cell phone, internet access) and that capital cities tend more to serve local service access better (water, sewerage, and electricity). The authors further study the (∪-shaped) relationship between city size and city performance, which shows that both small and large cities perform better than mid-size cities.

The authors show that citizens and firms generally benefit when their city provides an interface with technology, especially through the World Wide Web. Citizens and firms can leverage the information offered through web technology and may even use technology to self-provide their own services, particularly where there are obstacles to governance and globalization reforms at the city level. These new technologies may offer a partial substitute for a lack of political will to implement reforms by the public leadership in the city and country. New technologies, such as mobile phones and internet computing, enable private firms and city residents to effectively become more globalized on their own, independent of their city's performance. However, such a mitigating effect of technology can only be partial where governance and accountability is wanting, given the high mobility of residents, firms, and capital—they all have an "exit" option to leave the city for a better-performing one.

Furthermore, even as technological improvements will continue to provide individualized private solutions as substitutes for large-scale infrastructure provision, there always will be some services (given their economies of scale and indivisibility) for which the public sector will play an important role. For appropriate public and private-sector strategies, it becomes increasingly important for donor agencies and city managers alike to distinguish between different types of infrastructure services, depending on the technologies available and the particular characteristics of the city.

Policy Considerations and Further Research

Throughout this volume, the policy analysis is complicated by the interdependence between globalization and city performance: Do the demands of globalization produce better-performing cities, or is it the good performance of some cities that allows them to take advantage of the opportunities of globalization? This question of causality is crucial, so that policies can be designed to avoid the downward spiral in which cities that perform less well are not attractive for further globalization, and without the competitive pressures of globalization, poorly performing cities have less incentive to improve local governance. While the empirical evidence assembled here shows that per capita income and the degree of urbanization do play a role, as they explain many of the reasons for the improved performance of cities, city and national managers do have other kinds of leverage at the local level to improve city performance. Some cities in highly globalized countries, such as those in Eastern Europe—Ukraine is an example—and Africa—Nigeria, for instance—are in places where international investments have not made much of a dent in the low levels of city performance, economic growth, and quality of life. We suspect that the quality of city governance may be an important explanatory variable in this regard.

Time lag is also a vexing issue for understanding the relationship between globalization and urban performance. The impact of globalization is not felt overnight; there is some lag before results show up. Most of the data collated for this volume, compiling UN statistics from the early 1990s and an index of globalization indicators collected about a decade later for 62 countries, are somewhat out of date and out of synch, although they are the best information at hand. These data limitations make it difficult to draw valid conclusions on the impact of globalization on city behavior. Despite these weaknesses, however, the volume points to the benefits of empirically testing the various hypotheses on globalization and urbanization that may blindly guide current decision making. The paucity of data in this regard is a key obstacle to effective policy design at the national and subnational level. Efforts to improve the quality of data at the city level would go a long way to addressing this critical policy gap.

2

Globalization and Urban Infrastructure

Frannie Léautier and Andrew C. Lemer

Just north of the Dead Sea in the Jordan River's valley lies an archeological site popularly known as the city of Jericho. Excavations there have revealed evidence of human settlement that commenced some 11,000 years ago or earlier. By 10,000 years ago, the residents, perhaps 2,000 people living in mud-brick houses clustered in an area of 4 ha, sustained themselves by farming, hunting, and possibly herding sheep. Around their town they built walls, 1.5 m thick in places and today preserved to a height of about 4 m, with a moat-like ditch beyond. Into the wall they built a great circular stone tower 9 m in diameter.[1] This oldest of known human settlements had what we today would call civil infrastructure.[2]

Beginnings of Infrastructure

In his *Ten Books of Architecture,* written about 15 BC, the Roman Marcus Vitruvius Pollio declares that "A city's public buildings serve three purposes: defense, religion, and convenience. To ward off hostile attack, we must defend the city with walls, towers, and gates. For the sake of religion, we plan shrines, and sacred temples to the immortal gods. For convenience, we arrange public sites for general use—harbors, open spaces, colonnades, theaters, promenades, baths, and all amenities for like purpose. All," he famously instructs, "must be carried out with strength, utility, grace."[3] Infrastructure had clearly been recognized as an essential constituent of culture.

From such beginnings, our understanding of infrastructure has evolved. Nearly two millennia later, economist Adam Smith recognized the provision of public infrastructure as an essential foundation for the wealth of nations and—in sharp contrast to his views on most areas of human economic activity—one of the three essential duties of government.[4]

As the Industrial Revolution progressed, so did our theories on infrastructure. The French engineer and economist Jules Dupuit in the mid nineteenth century made important contributions to all aspects of infrastructure design and management, particularly with his ideas on ownership of the assets that infrastructure represents and how we should price their usage.[5]

Our recognition of the importance of pricing and its implications for how we finance infrastructure continued to grow as we came to understand the monopolistic power of government-based decision making and the implications for how scarce resources are allocated. American economist and statistician Harold Hotelling laid the groundwork for our understanding of how infrastructure influences regional patterns of economic activity and our treatment of such "exhaustible resources as energy supplies and environmental amenities (Hotelling 1929; Hotelling 1931).

Our concepts of infrastructure burst out of national boundaries with the founding of the World Bank in the aftermath of World War II's devastation. From its launch in 1945, the Bank was heavily involved in infrastructure development, including rehabilitation of India's railways, building power generation and transmission capacity in Brazil, Chile, and El Salvador, and similar activities around the world. The Bank's support for infrastructure was conceived as a critical means for building a foundation for long-term growth and social stability, and the discipline imposed by a focus on specific functions and facilities that infrastructure represented appealed to John Maynard Keynes and the other architects of the Bretton Woods system that underlies our modern economy.

The international comparison of infrastructure and its role in social and economic development yielded new insights. On the one hand, we have gained greater understanding that demand for infrastructure is a "derived demand." Infrastructure is desired not for its own sake but rather because it facilitates other economic and social activity. In regions at all levels of development, we have observed a statistically significant relationship between overall development and infrastructure,[6] and we surmise the correlation stems from infrastructure's real contributions to health, efficiency, and quality of life. On the other hand, as economist A. O. Hirschman concluded, the shortage that retards economic advance in most cases is management capability rather than physical facilities. Infrastructure is not a sufficient condition for development; it can be built later to "catch up" with demand derived from private industry's growth, but it is a necessary condition for further economic growth as there is no economy that has been able to grow in a sustainable way without infrastructure.[7]

Another hard lesson was laid out most clearly in Garrett Hardin's 1968 article in *Science*, "Tragedy of the Commons." Hardin used the example of primitive herdsmen who, seeking their own self interest, will be driven inexorably to build their herds and overgraze the shared grassland, to expound the conflicts inherent in efforts to encourage development when environmental amenities such as clean air and water are considered, for the most part, "free goods." While the concepts of public goods and externalities had been discussed among economists since early in the twentieth century,[8] Hardin's discussion used game theory and an accessible style to provide powerful impetus for the growth of environmental concerns in infrastructure management.

Globalization Emerges

The World Bank's founding and Hirschman's and Hardin's contributions to the literature are key markers of the progression within infrastructure of the broad economic trend we have come to call "globalization."[9] While the facilities and services of infrastructure are still seen by public work managers and users as essentially local, the underlying demands for infrastructure and the means employed in its finance and development are increasingly global in scope. Business relationships and production increasingly are spread across national boundaries. Work proceeds "24/7." Most important for increasing numbers of us who concern ourselves with infrastructure development and management, the ways we think about infrastructure and make decisions are undergoing fundamental changes.[10]

Transport and communications costs have declined tremendously over time further contributing to the globalization and integration of economies. Between 1920 and 1990, the average cost of freight and port charges declined from $95 per ton to $30 per ton. The cost of a three-minute phone call between London and New York declined from about $250 in 1940 to less than $1 in the 1990s. Computers cost about $12,000 in 1960 and now cost a few hundred dollars.

Our current infrastructure technology relies substantially on large production facilities tied together by fixed distribution links. Generating plants and wires, treatment plants and pipelines, "edge cities" and highways, and the like together compose geographically extensive networks; they entail large capital investments. Historians have argued that the basic pattern is rooted in the nineteenth century, but there have been remarkable advances in production and distribution capability—motorized vehicles, purified drinking water, electricity generation, to suggest only a few—that have greatly enhanced the services our infrastructure can provide (see, for example, Tarr and Dupuy 1988). The networks themselves have shown a remarkable capability for expansion, enabling delivery of services to once-remote areas. Service availability has, in turn, spurred further growth and spreading out of demand.

One of the first major indicators of infrastructure's globalization was the creation of Federal Express, incorporated in 1971. This transportation company's business model was a radical reinvention of the messenger services that supported all commerce prior to the advent of telecommunications. Fred Smith, the firm's founder, built on the existing air transport infrastructure to create the long-distance overnight delivery that has now become commonplace and expected. The ideas of manufacturers' stocking parts as needed in "just-in-time" inventories and moving partially finished goods from site to site to take advantage of local economies both owe their success to the insights embodied in FedEx.

The still-emerging impact of global cellular wireless telecommunications similarly is traceable to the 1973 U. S. patent application Martin Cooper and Motorola filed for a "radio telephone system." Cellular telephones have made it possible not only for business travelers to keep in touch easily with their offices, from almost anywhere in the world, but also for remote villages to link more effectively into the marketplace. The ability to manage a stream of global infrastructure services using local assets is hence enabled by global communication systems and the progress of infrastructure's globalization is further deepened by such technology.

Globalized infrastructure in turn influences globalized production. The low-cost digital watches that have become an immensely popular consumer product, often a fashion accessory, could not have been developed without global air transport and telecommunications. The 1976 introduction of the first $20 digital watch, by U. S. producer Texas Instruments highlighted the importance of labor costs in what had been a technology-based product. Prices dropped rapidly as production was moved out of North America. In less than a decade, only a single company (Timex) still assembled watches in the United States.

New global modes of infrastructure have emerged as well. The 1980 appearance of the CNN television network marked the arrival of a global information infrastructure that enabled dramatic change in how business is done. With global news and financial reporting delivered "real-time," all the time producers were brought closer than ever before to consumers and the sources of their factors of production.

Arguably more significant has been the accelerated global commerce in ideas, exemplified (for the authors, at least) by the 1989 fall of the Berlin Wall and the images of the events that were immediately available to viewers worldwide. Socialism essentially collapsed as a plausible model for the economic organization of human activities, and even those nations that continue to espouse Marxist social ideals are today adopting capitalist market mechanisms in progressively larger segments of their economies.

More subtly, the concept that infrastructure can be privately owned and operated without compromising public well-being has gained increasing acceptance, as exemplified by the 1990s transformation of water utilities in the United Kingdom. The necessary policy and regulatory reforms that were needed to support privately provided infrastructure progressed more rapidly in the telecommunications sector, partly due to the speed by which telecommunications systems were being integrated globally, with the increased needs for standards and compatibility also driving the need for common policy and institutional settings to provide, manage, and operate these systems. The more global integration of telecommunications, communication, and information services therefore resulted in a speeding up of the global provision and management of these systems, which still remained with important local infrastructures. In the water sector, where services remain to a large extent local, the progression of policy and institutional reform has also been much slower, as has been the penetration of globally managed water supply and sanitation systems. The water and telecommunications sector exemplify the acute factors that drive local versus global contrasts in infrastructure provision. Institutionally, the existence of regional integration attempts such as the European Union and Economic Commission of West African States (ECOWAS) illustrate further the need for common markets for infrastructure services such as transport, telecommunications, and energy that transcend the local nature of their assets.

With increasing private-sector participation has also come increasing internationalization of infrastructure management. The government approval in 1993 of an alliance between the Netherlands KLM and U. S.-based Northwest Airlines was an early case. The Wings Alliance, granted immunity from antitrust laws, represented a new institutional structure that circumvented ownership restrictions of predominant bilateral aviation agreements, which prevent mergers and acquisitions in international air transport. The alliance—and others that soon followed, such as United, Lufthansa, and SAS (forming the Star Alliance in 1997)—also represented a consequence of the U. S. government's Open Skies policy, which called for eliminating government restrictions on what routes airlines may fly, the number of flights they may schedule, and the fares they may charge. New Open Skies bilateral and multilateral treaties have created progressively larger free-trade zones in global air transport. The 1999 merger of France's Générale des Eaux with U. S. Filter Corporation to create Vivendi Environment, a multinational water company, represented a major extension of multinational management to water supplies.

The creation of the World Trade Organization (WTO) in 1995 institutionalized the goal of free trade and the ideal of collective action for the common good of all nations. Like the Berlin Wall, the WTO symbolizes a seismic change, particularly in establishing a binding dispute settlement system that is shaping our increasingly globalized infrastructure.

This progression of globalization has not been altogether smooth, of course. Infrastructure itself has become in more than a few cases an export industry, creating pockets of wealth held by the firms and employees who own and operate the infrastructure on which a widely dispersed and sometimes resentful consumer base relies for transport services, drinking water, energy, and waste disposal. Local communities also have shown increasing resentment and resistance to the presence of infrastructure facilities, even if those facilities could provide substantially improved services to the community. The English-language protest, "Not in my back yard," has evolved into the internationally recognized term "NIMBY." Because infrastructure draws on financial markets that have become global in scope, what might once have been local liquidity problems spill over into international affairs. Such financial upheavals as Mexico's "Tequila crisis" in the 1980s, Asia in the late 1990s, and more recently Turkey and Argentina have forced development economists to re-think the once-promising role of private financing in infrastructure development and management. The September 11, 2001, terrorist attack on the United States has invigorated and added international dimensions to discussions of local vulnerability and security. Such concerns have given rise to rethinking of the relationships of private and public interests in infrastructure service provision and highlighted the challenges for infrastructure professionals implied in the precept, "Think globally, act locally."[11]

Acting Locally

The essential challenge facing infrastructure professionals today is embodied in that precept. How are we to resolve the inherent—and seemingly inevitable—conflicts between accommodating individual interests versus serving collective preferences, and between meeting immediate demands versus providing for future generations. The resolution is achievable, if at all, only at the level of individual projects and enterprises. We offer several examples.

Overton Park, USA

Overton Park, a 138-ha city park located near the center of Memphis, Tennessee, in the United States, contains a zoo, a nine-hole municipal golf course, an outdoor theater, nature trails, an art academy, picnic areas, and 69 ha of forest. In 1956, local planners and the federal Bureau of Public Roads (now the Federal Highway Administration) proposed construction of a six-lane, high-speed, expressway cutting through the park, separating the zoo from the rest of the park and using some 10.5 ha of parkland for the new right-of-way. The road was planned as a segment of Interstate Highway 40, to provide a major east-west route through Memphis and easier access to downtown from the suburban areas on the city's eastern fringe. The design included primarily below-grade roadway running through open cuts, except for a segment crossing a stream. Government agencies acquired a right-of-way and announced final approval for the route and design in November 1969.

In the decades while the highway planners were at work, the postwar economic boom and rising middle-class prosperity in the United States were giving political strength to what we have come to call "environmental values." The National Environmental Policy Act (NEPA), passed by Congress at the end of 1969 and signed into law by President Nixon on January 1, 1970 (NEPA 1970), is arguably the most highly visible evidence of the changing balance of power, but there were other signs as well.

The Department of Transportation Act of 1966 included a crucial requirement in Section 4(f) prohibiting the Secretary of Transportation from authorizing the use of federal funds to finance the construction of highways through public parks if a "feasible and prudent" alternative route exists (DTA 1966). Only if no such route is available may the federal funding be authorized, and then only if the highway incorporates "all possible planning to minimize harm" to the park.

Residents of Memphis, confronted with the prospect of the new highway, formed protest groups and (indulging a strong inclination with U. S. society) hired lawyers. Acting through grass-roots organizations, they took the case to court, eventually reaching the U. S. Supreme Court.[12] They contended that announcements approving the route and design of I–40 did not include formal statements of the secretary of transportation's findings that there were no feasible and prudent alternative routes or that design changes could not be made to reduce the harm to the park.

In their court arguments, the citizen groups pointed out that routes around Overton Park certainly could be found. In addition, they argued, the current route could be followed by constructing the highway in a tunnel beneath the park, thereby substantially reducing the lasting adverse impact of cutting the park in two.

The planners responded that construction of a tunnel would greatly increase the cost of the project, create safety hazards, and increase in air pollution that would not reduce harm to the park. Lower courts had ruled in favor of the government's arguments that formal findings by the secretary of transportation were not necessary and that the secretary's authority was sufficiently wide to support his authorization of the construction.

The Supreme Court ruled in favor of the citizens groups. In doing so, the justices wrote:

> It is obvious that in most cases considerations of cost, directness of route, and community disruption will indicate that parkland should be used for highway construction whenever possible. Although it may be necessary to transfer funds from one jurisdiction to another, there will always be a smaller outlay required from the public purse when parkland is used since the public already owns the land and there will be no need to pay for right-of-way. And since people do not live or work in parks, if a highway is built on parkland no one will have to leave his home or give up his business. Such factors are common to substantially all highway construction. Thus, if Congress intended these factors to be on an equal footing with preservation of parkland there would have been no need for the statutes.
>
> Congress clearly did not intend that cost and disruption of the community were to be ignored by the Secretary. But the very existence of the statutes indicates that protection of parkland was to be given paramount importance. The few green havens that are public parks were not to be lost unless there were truly unusual factors present in a particular case or the cost or community disruption resulting from alternative routes reached extraordinary magnitudes.

The substantially increased costs that any alternative route or design would entail made federal funding of the project essentially impossible. Because federal funds paid for 95 percent of the construction costs of highways on the interstate system, eliminating federal funding effectively killed the project, and the highway was never built. The case was one of the earliest in which independent citizens groups had mobilized to oppose a government-sponsored project that had been planned according to established governmental procedures, and were successful. The case has been hugely influential, both as a citation in subsequent citizen actions to block other projects and as a force motivating the growth of broad public participation in the infrastructure investment process.

Chad-Cameroon Petroleum and Pipeline Development Project

A recent example similar to Overton Park is the Chad-Cameroon pipeline, a project to develop the oil fields in Doba in southern Chad (at a cost of US$ 1.5 billion) and construct a 1,070 km pipeline to offshore oil-loading facilities on Cameroon's Atlantic coast (US$ 2.2 billion). The project is intended to transform the economy of Chad, a country that is so poor at present, it cannot afford the minimum public services necessary for a decent life. By 2004, the pipeline would increase government revenues by 45–50 percent a year and allow it to use those resources for important investments in health, education, environment, infrastructure, and rural development, which are necessary to reduce poverty. The sponsors of the project exemplify what a globalized provision of infrastructure entails. Investments come from a consortium consisting of ExxonMobil of the United States (the operator, with 40 percent of the private equity), Petronas of Malaysia (35 percent), and Chevron-Texaco of the United States (25 percent). The project could result in nearly US$2 billion in revenues for Chad (averaging US$80 million a year) and US$500 million for Cameroon (averaging US$20 million a year) over the 25-year production period.[13]

This project had extensive environmental and social consultation, both at the local level with communities in Chad and Cameroon, but also internationally with concerned interests in environmental and social protection. Although the project has been seen as one of the best examples of how to manage the extraction benefits while preserving social and environmental heritage, it nevertheless faces challenges in dealing with potential corruption and ensuring transparency in the use of oil revenues. In addition to detailed country-specific work on environmental and social issues, this project also helped to launch cross-country work across the two countries. The two countries share a common vision for the project, they undertook similar analysis of alternatives, shared the same background work on biological studies and public health analysis, and followed the same approach to consultation and to dealing with oil spills.[14] However as chapters 3, 5, and 6 demonstrate, the process of engaging multiple stakeholders from civil society and the private sector is not an easy task. In spite of a well-designed consultation process, the project still faces governance challenges. Addressing problems of corruption requires constant vigilance and continued consultation.

Jamuna Bridge, Bangladesh

The Jamuna Bridge,[15] the eleventh longest bridge in the world, provides the first fixed crossing of the Jamuna River (the main channel of the Brahmaputra River in Bangladesh), linking the eastern and northwestern parts of Bangladesh. While the concept of the bridge was discussed as early as 1964, construction work commenced in October 1994, and the bridge opened to traffic in 1998, festooned with signs reading "Yesterday a dream, today a reality." With project costs of nearly

US$1 billion over a nine-year construction period, it was the most expensive and arguably the most challenging infrastructure investments ever undertaken in Bangladesh (World Bank 2000). The 4.8 km-long bridge itself is designed to serve multiple purposes, carrying a four-lane carriage way with shoulders and foundations adequate to carry a railway line, an electric power interconnector, a gas pipeline, and telecommunications facilities. In addition, the project entailed dikes and other complex river regulation for flood protection. Because of the river's braiding nature and concerns about the construction's impact on the changing morphology, the approximate location of the bridge could only be decided in late 1992 and the location of the bridge access roads could not be fixed until late 1994. Nearly 3,000 ha of land were acquired in a country where land is scarce, and some 100,000 people affected by the loss of agricultural land had to be helped.

The dream of the bridge had several aspects. Before the bridge, traders trucked and ferried fruits and vegetables from the northwest region to Dhaka and other markets on the more populous eastern banks, sometimes waiting days to cross the river and often arriving with their produce damaged or spoiled. Press reports quoted a local trader from the northwest, "There is a changing mentality here [with the bridge] . . . now Dhaka seems like it is next door." During devastating floods in 1998, the bridge played a critical role in preventing famine by enabling food and relief supplies to be transported quickly from one side of the country to the other. Government plans enabled by the bridge include development of new export processing zones and private tourism complexes on both sides of the river, which are expected to create jobs and reverse the rural-to-urban migration that has placed growing pressure on big cities such as Dhaka and Chittagong. As a crucial missing link in both the Asian Highway and the Trans-Asian Railway, the bridge is also opening new trade opportunities with neighboring countries. Traffic on the bridge has, for the most part, far exceeded expectation (Table 2.1).

By reducing the river's width at Kalihati from 12 km to 4.8 km, construction substantially reduced erosion that periodically destroyed homes along the river. A recent study indicates that at least 70 percent of the land along the Jamuna was permanently saved from erosion by the bridge's channeling effect. In addition, the electricity and gas interconnectors that are part of the project should relieve acute energy shortages in the northwest, where the only source of fuel has been firewood, as well as slowing deforestation and spurring growth of industry.

Although the technical aspects of the project were challenging, the institutional arrangements were even more challenging. Participants in decision making included local nongovernmental organizations (NGOs) involved in aid and economic development work, the people living in areas that would feel the impact of construction and changes in the patterns of river flow, the international and domestic firms that formed a joint venture and entered into a five-year contract to manage the operation of the toll bridge, the Inspection Panel appointed to ensure that the project met standards established by the World Bank Group, the Asian Development Bank, and the United Nations Development Programme. The Jamuna Bridge Authority (JMBA) was created by special legislation (the Jamuna Bridge Surcharge and Levy Ordinance), and given autonomous financial and managerial decision-making authority. Government agencies developed and put into effect an Environmental Management Action Plan, an Erosion and Flood Action Plan to mitigate impact, and a Resettlement Action Plan establishing legal rights to land and titles for fishing and families dependent on wildlife. Additional legislation facilitated

Table 2.1. Usage of the Jamuna Multipurpose Bridge

Measure of usage	Trucks	Buses	Light vehicles	Total or average
Average annual daily traffic in opening year	920	799	575	2,294
Growth rate, 1993–98 (percent)	3.6	24.1	32.7	18.1
Difference between appraisal and actual average annual daily traffic (percent)	−16.0	135.0	193.0	41.0

Source: World Bank 2000.

land acquisition and prevented speculators from making fraudulent claims for the loss of houses or structures.

The process employed to make decisions during the construction phase was also complex. Eight Milestone Decision Meetings were held over the course of project implementation, involving the Jamuna Multipurpose Bridge Authority, project financiers, a panel of experts appointed to advise on complex engineering, social, and environmental aspects of the project, representatives of the government of Bangladesh, consultants, contractors, and NGOs. There were also monthly meetings of the lenders to review progress.

The legislation, planning, and organization associated with the project represented a penetration of new ideas into a traditional and very low—income society. The degree to which Bangladeshis benefit from the project depends, in turn, on how effectively these ideas have changed weak local governance or built on its existing strengths. Residents of the city of Tangail on the eastern end of the bridge seem to have benefited more than the residents of Sirajganj on the west, for example, as measured by income increases. The fraction of people earning more than 5,000 taka per month in Tangail increased from 40 percent before the construction to 50 percent after, while in Sirajganj the fraction actually declined from 23 percent to 17 percent in the same period. Observers cite greater social cohesion in Tangail, support by local leadership for community development in surrounding villages, and lower incidence of conflict and fraud. In establishing land and property titles, the government registered title in both the husband and wife's names, thereby enhancing the status of women.[16]

After more than 40 years of planning and implementation, the Jamuna Bridge case shows how the inclusion of different stakeholders in decision making, commonly referred to as "empowerment," combined with the development of linkages among decentralized institutions, such as local and city governments, can introduce growth-enhancing infrastructure in a sustainable way. The project supports not only rural-to-urban trade and migration, but also global trade.[17] It was possible in the case of the Jamuna Bridge to see these results because of the length of time it took to get the project done and the complex consultations that were needed.

Deer Island Waste-Treatment Facility, Boston, USA

In part as a culmination of trends illustrated in our preceding examples, and in part because of the NIMBY problem that pervades infrastructure management, one of the most important trends we have observed is the development of infrastructure to always provide multiple services. Consider, for example, Boston's new sewage treatment facilities.

Notable as one of North America's oldest settlements, the city of Boston now lies at the hub of a sprawling region of some 3.4 million people working and living in 129 politically distinct communities. Years of what some people viewed as total neglect of the region's wastewater problems had turned Boston Harbor, by the late 1970s, into one of the United States' most polluted coastal water bodies. Poorly maintained and undersized treatment plants poured millions of tons of raw sewage into the harbor, exposing neighboring communities to health hazards and foul odors. Funding that might have paid for improvements was a low priority for politically driven public officials. Motivated initially by a court suit filed by one of the coastal jurisdictions and encouraged by the federal Environmental Protection Agency (EPA), the state of Massachusetts in 1984 created a new institution, the Massachusetts Water Resource Authority (MWRA), to supply water and sewer services to 61 communities.

Almost immediately, the EPA filed suit against the MWRA for violations of the federal Clean Water Act's limits on pollution. The suit was motivated, according to staff members involved at the time, by concerns that no local constituencies had yet formed and there seemed to be no political leadership for action (Grant and Lemer 1993). A court-ordered schedule of actions required to bring the MWRA into compliance with the act included consolidation of waste treatment operations, construction of new primary and secondary waste-treatment facilities at the authority's Deer Island plant, and construction of a 15-km tunnel outfall, 7.3 m in diameter, to carry treated effluent beyond the harbor into Massachusetts Bay. The decade-long construction project commenced in 1989. The Boston Harbor Project capital investment program as a whole will cost an estimated $7.1 billion by the time it is completed in 2009.

The enormous cost of the project results in part from its expansive objectives. If the purpose were only to eliminate the pollution pouring into the water, a local engineering professor surmised, refitting every house in the region with a modern low-volume toilet and building a smaller treatment plant would have done as well and cost substantially less. The various community, local governments, and federal agencies sought to ensure, among other objectives, that whales in Massachusetts Bay and beach-goers on the northern shore of Cape Cod would be unaffected by the project, at least in the long term.

The environmental and social resources thereby invested in the project—aquatic biota and recreational attractions—are secured by technology paid for by the region's municipal water consumers: 90 percent of project funds will be provided by local sources. The *Christian Science Monitor* reported that homeowners' water bills increased 329 percent between 1986 and 1999. Annual water charges per household were projected to reach $1,002 by 2005. However, the treatment plant's location on Deer Island offers attractive views of Boston Harbor, the downtown skyline, and airplanes flying to and from Boston's Logan Airport. The MWRA has included walking trails and other amenities for the region's residents, which go beyond the project's immediate scope and boost the total return on investment.

Distributed Energy in Uganda and the Multi-Utilities

Despite the democratizing influence that the Overton Park, Chad-Cameroon Pipeline, and the Jamuna Bridge projects had through their involvement of many voices not typically heard in the infrastructure decision-making process, all three projects were relatively traditional in their centralized concentration of resources and effort. A somewhat different perspective emerges from the case of rural electrification in Uganda. New technologies for renewable energy sources—solar energy using photovoltaics and thermal conversion, biomass conversion, wind, and small-scale hydroelectric generation—have been coupled with institutional reforms to allow small-scale enterprises to provide power outside of the network grids. Furthermore, a role for small communities to provide their own energy supplies has allowed two previously separate markets—undersupplied rural areas and off-grid industries and farms, and expanding peripheral neighborhoods in congested urban locations—to converge, to their mutual benefit.

Uganda has a population of 23 million people, nearly 5 million households, but only about 10 percent have access to electricity. Most of those with access live in the capital city of Kampala. Rural and periurban Ugandans make up for lack of access to electricity by using other forms of energy, including kerosene, dry-cell batteries, lead-acid car batteries, and self-generating sets (Table 2.2). Ugandans spend an estimated US$ 100 million per year to power radios, cassette players, and flashlights, indicating that there is a potentially large market for low-cost alternative energy supplies. Recognition of that potential provided the incentive for the government of Uganda to make regulatory and institutional changes.

Prior to these changes, all energy-related business in the country was controlled by the Uganda Electricity Board, established in 1948 as a quasi-independent, vertically integrated monopoly to generate, transmit, distribute, and supply electricity within Uganda and to its neighboring countries. In 1999, the Electricity Act was passed which (a) removed the Uganda Electricity Board monopoly in the power sector; (b) unbundled generation, transmission, and distribution of electricity services into separate companies; and (c) established an independent sector regulator and created a legal and regulatory framework for private sector participation in the energy sector. This reform allowed the emergence of independent power producers to deliver services by accessing the main grid for supply of rural areas, developing independent grid systems, and using the potential of solar or other alternative supplies. The reform allowed fair competition of all suppliers and the use of regionally differentiated retail rates and tariffs, as well as nondiscriminatory wheeling and access tariffs to facilitate power transactions between distribution concessionaires and third party generators. Subsidy transfer and financing mechanisms were also instrumental.

Table 2.2. *Alternative Sources of Energy and Their Costs for Ugandan Residents*

Energy source	Monthly cost to the household (USh)	Share of households using the source (percent)	Cost (US$/Kwh)
Kerosene	5,000	100	
Dry-cell batteries	6,000	94	400
Lead-acid car batteries	10,900	9	3
Aggregate cost per year			
Self-generating set	$19 million		0.19

Note: USh 1050 = US$1 (as of September 1997).
Source: World Bank 2001; World Bank 1999.

The government put in place a system to support renewable supply development, using the World Bank—executed Global Environmental Facility (GEF) to support stand-alone solar photovoltaics. The Bank's Prototype Carbon Fund was used to finance the development of cogeneration capacity at sugar mills and coffee husking facilities, as well as the use of small and mini hydro generation and wind generation. The fund was also used to offer financial support for private sector, commercially oriented development of energy distribution services to rural and periurban areas.

The approach to distributed provision for energy in Uganda also allowed the development of other utility services in a distributed manner, offering opportunities for companies to offer multi-utility solutions. These included telephone services for accelerated rural access to basic telephone, the spread of internet services to district capitals, as well as the development of pilot telecenters. This experience is mirrored in the emergence, in several countries, of "multi-utilities," companies that offer a range of bundled utilities including electric power, natural gas, water and sewerage, and telephone service.[18]

Starpower in the metropolitan Washington, DC, area is an example of a company offering bundled services in telephone, cable, and internet.[19] In the United Kingdom, bundled gas and electricity services as well as electricity and water are common. Other countries with bundled utility services include Argentina, Cape Verde, Colombia, Costa Rica, and Morocco. In some countries, the bundling extends even beyond utility services. For example, in Hungary a single company offers both transport and telecommunications, while in Chile it is combination of gas and telecommunications services.

Regulatory reform that permits such integration of services is one key factor motivating these enterprises, but efficiencies gained by horizontal integration is another. These companies seek to take advantage of their existing networks of government and customer relations, financing capacity, administrative services, and use of buildings, equipment, and network rights of way. A multi-utility strategy can also be pursued as companies look for opportunities for vertical integration, such as bundling generation and distribution services in the power sector, or linking exports at a port with hinterland transport and then to a bundled port and rail service. P&O Company, which has invested in the Port of Colombo in Sri Lanka as well as in other countries, pursues such a strategy.

Dimensions of Infrastructure Globalization

Such examples as these illustrate four broad dimensions of change characterizing the evolution of globalized infrastructure (Table 2.3), an evolution toward more effectively resolving conflicts between individual and collective interests, and between people's immediate demands and society's desire to provide for future generations.

Democratization

When the environmentally minded citizens of Memphis and the villagers and farmers along the Jamuna River became a part of the decision making that shaped a major infrastructure investment, they exemplified a broad trend of *democratization* in the decision-making process. Clever use of the political process, requirements

Table 2.3. *Dimensions of Infrastructure Globalization*

Dimension	Manifestations of change
Democratization of management	• Citizen participation in infrastructure development • Distributed ownership of infrastructure and its returns • Environmental movement as force in infrastructure management
Decentralization of service provision	• High-occupancy vehicle (HOV) operating on roads as preferred alternative to rail transit • Wind power and small-scale power producers • Agency reform/restructuring
Diffusion of innovation	• Private provision of public services, build-own-operate development, warrantees, and maintenance contracting • Cellular telephone standards • Water-system megacorps – City to City exchange of knowledge, services, and ideas
Diversification of service scope	• Debt-for-environment swaps • Investments for historic preservation, world cultural resources, and other "nonmarket" goods • "Green" accounting

imposed by delay-averse financiers, and pressures of world opinion have motivated inclusion of a wider range of "stakeholder" interests in infrastructure investment and operations. Viewed from the global perspective, we believe this trend is the consequence for infrastructure of general political movements toward more open societies.

Decentralization

The emergence of small-scale producers and a distributed supply system in Uganda's power sector illustrates a general trend toward *decentralization* we observe on the supply side of infrastructure worldwide. Infrastructure management is devolving toward less centralized control and smaller-scale production processes enabled by new technologies. The immense success of the automobile (and of motorcycles in those places where incomes remain low) reflects an early instance of the trend now most apparent in energy supply, and perhaps telecommunications. We foresee advances in waste treatment and recycling that could spur similar changes in the water sector.

Diffusion

New, good ideas have always spread by *diffusion* from one user to others in different regions or fields of activity, but the speed and transnational scale of the transfers we are seeing in infrastructure mark a third important dimension of globalizing infrastructure. The rise of multinational infrastructure providers willing and prepared to operate and perhaps even retain ownership shares as well as plan and build infrastructure in other countries represents a major shift from the historical willingness of investors to lend money across borders. In addition, the development of cadres of professionals in many places, educated at a relatively few world-class institutions, has both facilitated the spread of ideas and provided the intellectual resources needed to adapt those ideas to the specific conditions of site and situation. The ability to communicate easily using video conferencing, e-mail, and the internet, as well as the ease of international travel, are facilitating this diffusion; the World Bank Group, for example, has brought together in a virtual meeting mayors from cities and towns throughout Brazil and international experts, for a day of live discussions of new ideas on city management and development.[20]

Diversification

As we have already suggested, the trend toward *diversification*—expansion of the range of services expected of infrastructure—has been motivated in no small measure by the increased difficulty of putting new infrastructure into service. This increasing difficulty is in turn attributable, at least in part, to the trend toward democratization in decision making. However, it reflects also a shift in the values people judge to be important for making decisions; higher priority is now given to protection of wildlife habitat and social stability of communities, for example, than might have been the case several decades ago. We are broadening our concept of the "capital" invested in infrastructure, as well, now recognizing that pristine streams, close-knit neighborhoods, and historic structures have resource value that may not be fully reflected in current market prices. Gradually we are finding ways to measure these resources and make them more fungible, for example trading financial debt for protection of unique lands, or the exchanging pollution rights through the World Bank's nascent Carbon Trading System.

Institutions for the Continuing Evolution of Infrastructure

We are confident that the trends of infrastructure globalization will and should continue. We anticipate then that infrastructure professionals will more and more be called upon to think globally while acting locally, through more open decision making, less centralized control, use of internationally best and latest practices, and provision of diverse multiple services using fewer resources.

The traditional owners and developers of infrastructure, local governments and their consultants who must answer primarily to their local electorate, are not well prepared to deal with the challenges of globalized infrastructure. We foresee a growing need for institutions that can facilitate collective action in infrastructure development and management. Such institutions will supplement traditional government agencies, elected officials, and infrastructure professionals by enhancing decision makers' sensitivity to the indicators of local communities' concerns, including communities at the fringe, and facilitating the balancing of different groups' interests, including those of future generations, and executing and implementing agreed decisions with commitment and accountability to all key stakeholders.

These institutions will have to operate at community, local, regional, national, and multinational levels, enabling coordination across boundaries, professions, and cultures. They will have to recognize and respect the hierarchy of interests that must be balanced in making globalized infrastructure management decisions. Individual preferences gain priority as democratization progresses, and these new institutions must provide the means for reaching consensus when many individuals and groups are influenced differently by infrastructure investment and operating decisions.

We see some emergent examples of what these new institutions might be. In addition to such multilateral political bodies as the WTO, environmental organizations such as the Nature Conservancy increasingly are working in cooperation with local governments and businesses to protect environmental resources while satisfying demands for infrastructure services. However, institution building takes time and there are many barriers to coordination. The new institutions we foresee will necessarily operate differently from today's practices.

In particular, the new management institutions will have to mitigate the risks posed by rising expectations and diffuse preferences. If individuals and groups expect to be pleased with all aspects of an infrastructure decision, they will almost certainly be disappointed. If institutions of collective action serve only to express that disappointment rather than to facilitate the balance of interests that leads to consensus, decisions will be thwarted instead of implemented. We need to expand our working concepts of what is fair and just in managing infrastructure and make those concepts an effective part of the decision-making process.

As we do so, we will need to devise new ways of exercising management and regulatory control of infrastructure. We certainly can be more effective in the pricing of infrastructure services when markets exist, but we need also to continue developing tools to assist us when markets do not function.

Finally, and most fundamental, we need the motivation to keep working toward infrastructure supportive of sustainable long-term growth and improvement in our quality of life. As infrastructure professionals, we have a commitment to humanity's future prosperity and a belief in our capacity for improvement. At the same time, we recognize that people may disagree on the precise meanings of such terms—prosperity, improvement, and the like—and how they are to be achieved. Without question, infrastructure's globalization poses great and growing challenges for the people who work to manage that infrastructure, but for us the rewards to be gained by meeting those challenges make the effort well worthwhile.

Notes

1. The purposes of Jericho's infrastructure may not have been entirely military; see, for example Bar-Yosef 1986, pp. 157–62.

2. There is not a universally accepted definition of "infrastructure," which some prefer to call "civil infrastructure," "public-works infrastructure," or simply "public works." To confuse matters further, the computer industry has in recent years adopted the word to refer to a variety of software and hardware that enable companies to keep track of their inventory, sales, personnel, and other business information. We confine ourselves to the more traditional usage, but take an inclusive view, that infrastructure encompasses facilities and services provided by government and the private sector. A committee of the U. S. National Research Council referred to "public works infrastructure" as including "both specific functional modes—highways, streets, roads, and bridges; mass transit; airports and airways; water supply and water resources; wastewater management; solid-waste treatment and disposal; electric power generation and transmission; telecommunications; and hazardous waste management—and the combined system these modal elements comprise. A comprehension of infrastructure spans not only these public works facilities, but also the operating procedures, management practices, and development policies that interact together with societal demand and the physical world to facilitate the transport of

people and goods, provision of water for drinking and a variety of other uses, safe disposal of society's waste products, provision of energy where it is needed, and transmission of information within and between communities" (National Research Council 1987). The World Bank describes infrastructure as an "umbrella term for many activities referred to as 'social overhead capital'" by development economists; the World Bank concentrates on "economic infrastructure," meaning services from public utilities, public works, and other transport sectors. (World Bank 1994).

3. While the text translation as "buildings" has made this quotation a favorite of architects, Vitruvius's inclusion of walls, harbors, and open spaces makes clear the broader scope of his interest and the relevance of his advice for the professions of engineering and others that have in modern times become less comfortable with grace as a design value to be weighed against strength and utility.

4. Smith writes in *Book Five of An Inquiry into the Nature and Causes of the Wealth of Nations*, published in 1776, "The third and last duty of the sovereign or common-wealth is that of erecting and maintaining those public institutions and those public works which, though they may be of the highest degree advantageous to a great society, are, however, of such a nature that the profit could never repay the expense to any individual or small number of individuals, and which it cannot be expected that any individual or small number of individuals should erect or maintain. The performance of this duty requires, too, very different degrees of expense in the different periods of society."

5. Dupuit's work earned him the Légion d'honneur in 1843; he published several significant contributions in the *Annales des Ponts et Chaussées*. See, for example, International and Economic Papers, 1952.

6. Many researchers have looked at the relationship between infrastructure and economic growth using a number of measures of infrastructure. We have in mind here the type of work done by Canning and Bennathan (2000), "The Social Rate of Return of Infrastructure Investments," and Charles Hulten (1997), "The Contribution of Infrastructure to Aggregate Output," both reviewed in Abstracts of Current research in Infrastructure produced by the World Bank's Development Economics Department. This work made very specific advances in the use of analytical and empirical models for quantifying the contribution of infrastructure to economic development.

7. Hirschman's seminal 1958 book, *The Strategy of Economic Development,* was followed in 1967 by his Development Projects Observed. The latter book motivated a rethinking of the World Bank's programs, and Hirschman's work generally encouraged aid organizations to focus on international exchange of students and technical services. See also Gillis and others 2001.

8. English economists Alfred Marshall and his student Arthur Pigou are most closely identified with the principles that underlie much of modern environmental economics.

9. *New York Times* columnist Thomas L. Friedman is given much of the credit for popularizing the term and defining the forces and attitudes it entails, for example, in his best-selling book, *The Lexus and the Olive Tree: Understanding Globalization* (Friedman 1999).

10. Indeed, we argue that a new globalized infrastructure profession has emerged. *Infrastructure professionals* are concerned with the planning, design, finance, construc-

tion, management, and operation of the public's fixed capital assets, without necessarily specializing in the workings of any single functional service area, such as water supply, transport, or waste management. As with infrastructure itself, there is disagreement about whether there truly can be "infrastructure professionals," as we characterize ourselves, or only specialists who have wandered outside of their areas of competence.

11. This phrase has been widely adopted as a slogan for activism in many areas. Its origin lies, we believe, in economist E. F. Schumacher's seminal book, *Small Is Beautiful: Economics as if People Mattered* (Schumacher 1973).

12. Citizens To Preserve Overton Park, Inc., et al., v. John A. Volpe, Secretary, Department of Transportation, et al., 1971 (401 U.S. 402, 91 S.CT. 814).

13. More details about the Chad-Cameroon Project can be found in http://www.worldbank.org/afr/ccproj.

14. Among the detailed analyses and studies done for this project are the Chad Environmental Management Plan, Compensation and Resettlement Plan, Regional Development Plan, Waste Management Plan, and Environmental Line List and Alignment Sheets. The Cameroon-specific volumes include the Environmental Management Plan, Compensation Plan, Environmental Foundation Plan, which encompasses an indigenous peoples plan and the offsite environmental enhancement program, Waste Management Plan, and Environmental Line List, and Alignment Sheets.

15. The bridge has been officially named, by a decision of the Bangladeshi National Parliament, the Bangabandhu Jamuna Bridge, in honor of the first prime minister of the independent nation.

16. However, the enhanced status of women also resulted in higher demands for dowry.

17. *World Development Report 2003* on Sustainable Development refers to the kind of institutions needed to perform certain functions well: pick up signals and diagnose problems early and from the fringes—requiring feedback, information, and voice; balance interests—requiring transparency and open fora for discussion; and execute agreed decisions and implement them-requiring credible commitments and accountability (World Bank 2003). The Jamuna bridge case shows that these types of institutions can be created, but they take time (60 years in the case of the Jamuna Bridge from concept to opening up for traffic) and are fragile.

18. While the Distributed Energy Project in Uganda is a good case for the multiutility concept, it is not easy to generalize from it. At the time this case was written, the project had just become effective and little had been achieved in terms of intended development objectives.

19. Starpower is a telecommunications company only, but it does indicate the manner in which companies are leveraging their customer interface and common rights of way to deliver an otherwise expensive infrastructure service. Such companies as Bechtel, Fluor, Lyonnaise des Eaux and Indosuez are have grown from their roots in construction to become multinational providers of infrastructure services.

20. The virtual conference, in December 2002, was enabled by an investment by the government of Brazil, corporations in Brazil such as Banco do Brasil, and the World Bank, in a Distance Learning Network commonly known as the Global Development Learning Network (GDLN).

References

Bar-Yosef, O. 1986. "Walls of Jericho: An Alternative Interpretation." *Current Anthropology* 27(2): 157–62.

Department of Transportation Act. 1966. P. L. 89–670, as amended; 49 USC 1653, Subtitle 1, Section 303(c).

Friedman, Thomas L. 1999. *The Lexus and the Olive Tree: Understanding Globalization.* New York: Farrar, Straus and Giroux.

Gillis, Malcolm, Dwight H. Perkins, and Michael Roemer. 2001. *Economics of Development.* 5th ed. London: Norton.

Grant, A. A., and A. C. Lemer, eds. 1993. *In Our Own Backyard: Principles for Effective Improvement of the Nation's Infrastructure.* Washington, DC: National Academy Press.

Hirschman, A.O. 1958. *The Strategy of Economic Development.* New Haven: Yale University Press.

———. 1967. *Development Projects Observed.* Washington, DC: Brookings Institution Press.

Hotelling, Harold. 1929 "Stability in Competition." *Economic Journal* 39: 41–57.

———. 1931 "The Economics of Exhaustible Resources." *Journal of Political Economy* 39(2): 137–75.

International and Economic Papers. 1952. "On the Measurement of the Utility of Public Works," by Jules Dupuit, originally published in 1844, reproduced in translation in International and Economic Papers 2: 83–110. London: Macmillan.

National Research Council. 1987. *Infrastructure for the 21st Century.* Washington, DC: National Academy Press.

NEPA (National Environmental Protection Act). 1970. P. L. 91–190, as amended; 42 USC 4321–4347.

Schumacher, E. F. 1973. *Small Is Beautiful: Economics as if People Mattered* London: Blond and Briggs.

Tarr, Joel A., and Gabriel Dupuy, eds. 1988. *Technology and the Rise of the Networked City in Europe and America.* Philadelphia : Temple University Press.

World Bank. 1994. *World Development Report 1994: Infrastructure for Development.* New York: Oxford University Press.

———. 1999. "Uganda-Rural Electrification Strategy study." Energy Sector Management Assistance Programme (ESMAP). September 1999.

———. 2000. "Implementation Completion Report for the Jamuna Bridge Project." June 19, 2000.

———. 2001. "Uganda Energy and Rural Transformation Project." PID 9031.

———. 2003. *World Development Report 2003: Sustainable Development.* New York: Oxford University Press.

3

Globalization and Urban Performance

Daniel Kaufmann, Frannie Léautier, and Massimo Mastruzzi

Does the impact of globalization at the city and country level matter for sound urban governance? Do sound urban governance and globalization affect city performance?

While studies on the first question are particularly scarce, some insights into the second question can be found in the existing literature. In particular, there has been an explosion in the literature on globalization and urban management. A simple search on the internet reveals thousands of citations and references on the topic. These range from theoretical explorations, such as the work of the Globalization and World Cities Group (GaWC) based in Loughborough University, England, to journalistic pieces that refer to specific decisions made by cities to position themselves in a global world. The work of Saskia Sassen dominates the citations on the subject of globalization and cities, and a number of sites dedicate themselves to organizing the literature and the data on globalization with some reference to cities, such as the work of the Transnationalism Project of the University of Chicago. The most frequently used term to refer to the globalization of cities is "networked," followed by "flows," both of which appear in the vast majority of the internet searches. However, references to globalization in the sense of world cities appear in only 3 percent of the citations—and even much sparser are references to governance.[1]

The virtual absence of data and empirically based treatment of the subject is particularly striking. A search of the empirical literature on globalization and urban governance suggests a significant gap, largely due to limited comparable cross-city data. This is particularly the case on governance and globalization issues, where an internet-based search elicits very few empirically based entries. Researchers have in fact lamented the difficulty of getting reliable comparative data to analyze the issues related to globalization of cities (see Short and others 1996 and Knox 2002).

But do the data at our disposal permit even an initial exploration into those issues at the city level? If so, is there significant variation in city-level performance, governance, and globalization—even within countries? Are differences across cities significant enough to warrant this line of empirical inquiry? And even if they are, do these differences matter? Within this initial empirical exploration, we try to address these issues. We find that the cross-city variance worldwide is rather substantial; in fact even within countries such intracity variance is not small—in general the extent of within-country cross-city variance is above one-half the cross-country variation. Such apparent rich diversity of experiences and performance across cities is worth reviewing, and thus exploring the potential determinants of the variation in performance is warranted.

Consequently, in this chapter we try to contribute to the field of urban governance and globalization through an empirically based exploration of some key determinants of the performance of cities. This empirical inquiry is made possible through the construction of a worldwide database for cities that contains variables and indicators of globalization (at the country and city level), city governance, and city performance (access and quality of service delivery). This city database integrates existing data with new data gathered specifically for this research project.[2]

The next section, City Performance in the Context of Globalization, provides a discussion of conceptual and definitional issues on city globalization, providing a partial survey of the literature. In the section, Urban Governance in the Context of Globalization, we review some of the relevant literature to capture the dynamics of city performance. The section on Determinants of City Performance provides simplified hypotheses on the globalization and governance nexus in explaining city-level performance in terms of service delivery, includes a working definition of urban governance, and presents a reduced-form model specification to test key hypotheses. That section also describes the extended city level dataset we have compiled, comprising data on 412 cities in 134 countries, from which we use more than 35 variables.[3] We also present in brief the results, both in terms of simple summary charts synthesizing the uncontrolled correlations, as well as the econometric specifications and the synthesis of the econometric results of the determinants of city performance. Given the extensive set of variables in the dataset, and multiple econometric specifications, we present synthesis tables and graphs summarizing the main econometric results. In the section, Determinants of City Governance, we present the results of the preliminary empirical investigation of the factors that potentially determine city governance. Future research questions are dealt with in the concluding section, where we also present emerging policy implications from this analysis.

City Performance in the Context of Globalization

There are two main threads in the literature that treat the subject of globalization of cities, which mostly refer to the term "world city" to describe the phenomenon. We take the theoretical underpinnings of this definition from the work of Doel and Hubbard (2002), who clarify key definitions and develop the conceptualization of globalization of cities. The two concept that we draw from include the following definitions:

- Globalized City as a *place:* a city is a location within the world, defined with precise city boundaries, but plugged into global flows, such as foreign direct investment that comes along with the decisions companies make to locate in particular cities, as well as the flow of people who come to work for these companies or visit for business purposes and the flow of goods and services that are produced by these companies as they decide to locate in a particular city. In such a definition, a global city would get value out of its indigenous characteristics, such as its past investments in critical infrastructure and the quality of its institutions. Such a city would also get benefits from the decisions of companies to locate in that city and conduct economic activities, such as banking, finance, accounting, legal services, or advertising. Urban politicians and city managers would be concerned about bringing local value to their citizens, reacting to global events that affect the city and creating strategies to adapt the city to best advantage. They would therefore be seeking to attract such companies or make sure they stay in the city, providing the key inputs and incentives such firms and their related personnel would need.

- Globalized City as a sustained achievement of *performance:* a city is a provider of services to its citizens, which can be measured by the quality of its services (access to telephone services, water, sewerage, or electricity), the reliability of such services over time (as measured by the quality of infrastructure services), and the degree to which a city involves its citizens in decision making, is responsive to their demands, and is well governed in general. Such a city would have relationships with other cities and key players in the global economy, including the people, firms, and organizations that are distributed across the world-city network. Urban politicians would strive to sustain good performance and would interact with citizens and firms to make choices on investment at the city level and to ensure the delivery of key services. How such politicians govern is as important as what services they deliver in such a definition.

The first definition of a globalized city refers to cities that are international leaders, are externally oriented toward a global economy, have a high ranking in the world's urban hierarchy, or serve as a major gateway for migration. Such cities have existed as far back as the sixteenth century. Knox (2002) highlights the shift that cities have experienced in how they have organized trade or geopolitical strategies beyond their boundaries. Cities such as London, Amsterdam, Antwerp, Genoa, Lisbon, and Venice were key global players in the seventeenth century. In the eighteenth century, Paris, Rome, and Vienna became main players in the world, while Antwerp and Genoa lost influence. In the nineteenth century, Venice lost some of its influence while cities such as Berlin, New York, and St. Petersburg joined the league of world cities. The shifting in and out of global influence, demonstrated by the example of Genoa, however, supports the second definition of a globalized city, as an outcome of decisions made by firms and individuals, which we wish to explore. We would like to investigate empirically what determines the staying power of cities in their performance on a global scale and whether governance has anything to do it.

Empirical analyses that have been done using the first definition of a globalized city—a city as a place interacting with the global space—have included a number of indicators, including the seven defined by Friedman (1986): (a) the financial assets of a city, such as its capital and equity markets; (b) the principal infrastructure that would influence the decisions of firms and citizens to locate in the city, exit to alternative options, or push to get governance reforms that would allow them to receive improved services;[4] (c) the size of the city in terms of its population and economies of scale; (d) the availability and concentration of key business services and advanced producer services, such as credit rating, risk management, and multijurisdictional law; (e) the city's manufacturing output; (f) the presence of transnational corporations, especially those that have located their headquarters in the city; and (g) the presence of international institutions in the city.

Other authors have used indicators such as the presence of internet domain names (Townsend 2001); the extent of public-private partnerships (Kresl 1995); measures of cultural vitality (Smith and Timberlake 1995); the proportion of foreign residents in the city (Doel and Hubbard 2002); and the numbers of service sector employees in the city (Doel and Hubbard 2002).

Very few authors have carried out empirical investigation using the second definition of globalized cities, which considers scale (the size of a city, its economy, or its private sector activity) or services (access to infrastructure and social services) as something produced rather than given, requiring cities to constantly perform to remain influential in a global world. New literature that focuses on the connectivity of cities within a network includes that of Sassen (2000), Castells (2000), and Doel and Hubbard (2002). Uncovering the variables that drive the dynamics of city growth and performance interests us, and we particularly look at the role of governance, using a set of empirical tests (see Chapter 6 as well).

From the data we have been able to gather from various sources, we can look at the effect of both the scale of the city and the quality of services and investigate the hypotheses developed by Friedman (1986) and Townsend (2001).[5]

In latter sections, we develop and implement a simple framework to study empirically the potential determinants of urban performance, within which globalization is hypothesized to be an important factor. From that perspective, we are to view the two definitions of a globalized city as complementary rather than as alternative hypotheses. Simply, the first definition of a globalized city (particularly regarding companies' decisions to locate in the cities and conduct economic activities, such as banking, finance, accounting, legal services, or advertising) is to be seen as a potential input to sound urban performance, while the second definition (particularly regarding the achievement of performance, including service delivery and quality of governance) is to be seen as the output or outcome of various inputs (including whether the city is global or not). In this respect, to avoid a quasi-tautology, we move away from equating the second view with a global city, instead regarding it simply as urban performance outcomes.[6]

We therefore posit the simple view that the two definitions of a global city are not necessarily substitutes or competing with each other, but potentially complementary, the first notion potentially being a determinant of city performance. Such a construction builds on the Tiebout (1956) hypothesis of "voting with your feet" and allows us to accept endogeneity. A city with good performance in terms of amenities it provides to its citizens (schools, health services, parks) attracts more migrant residents who "vote" to locate there. Such cities would therefore grow in size and, if the size of a city gives it advantage in a global world, the issue of "performance" may have an endogenous component, similarly with respect to location of firms. The dynamics of such a construct dictate that well performing cities would be well managed and hence even better performing.

Urban Governance in the Context of Globalization

In the recent past, much work has been done on globalization and on governance at the country level. While this is not the main focus of the chapter (and thus we do not provide a literature review), it is of relevance to briefly review the notions of governance and globalization at the country level for two reasons: first, as background to these same twin notions, but at the city level, which will be covered in more detail; second, because country-level variables may also significantly affect city-level performance.

Governance and Globalization at the Country Level: Basic Definitions

We have defined country-level governance as the exercise of authority through formal and informal traditions and institutions for the common good, thus encompassing: (a) the process of selecting, monitoring, and replacing governments; (b) the capacity to formulate and implement sound policies and deliver public services, and (c) the respect of citizens and the state for the institutions that govern economic and social interactions among them. The three dimensions in this definition of governance are then further unbundled to comprise two measurable concepts per dimension, for a total of six components:

- *Voice and external accountability* (such as the government's preparedness to be externally accountable through citizen feedback, democratic institutions, and a competitive press)
- *Political stability and lack of violence, crime, and terrorism*
- *Government effectiveness* (including quality of policy making, bureaucracy, and public service delivery)
- *Lack of regulatory burden*
- *Rule of law* (protection of property rights, judiciary independence, and so on)
- *Control of corruption.*

These components are subject to empirical measurement at the country level, for which a worldwide dataset has been constructed (Kaufmann, Kray, and Mastruzzi 2003).

Defining Urban Governance

Although the literature search found fewer citations that give access to specific empirical data sets, it revealed no lack of citations on the definition and use of the term "urban governance." UNESCO defines urban governance as the processes that steer and take into account the various links between stakeholders, local authorities, and citizens. It involves bottom-up and top-down strategies to favor active participation of concerned communities, open negotiation among actors, transparent decision making, and innovative urban management policies (UNESCO 2000). More comprehensively, Mehta and the UN Centre for Human Settlements define urban governance and describe potential indicators of urban governance (Mehta 1998 and UNCHS 1999).

Mehta (1998) looks at urban governance through a set of attributes. He introduces the attribute of *accountability*, which he suggests is derived from how cities manage their finances, communicate on use of funds and achievements to their citizens, and adhere to legal requirements and administrative policies. Embedded in Mehta's concept of accountability is the question of *responsiveness*, which includes the ability of a decentralized entity to determine and respond to the needs of its constituents. In doing so, city officials need to have processes of citizen *participation* and a system for monitoring and evaluation, as well as a means of reporting on results achieved. These three measures are critical if one is using the definition of a city as a place, because they indicate a city's performance with respect to local issues and skill in managing the consequences of globalization locally.

If we consider the other definition of a globalized city, as an outcome of globalization but also shaping the city's role within a globalized world, then we need to look at dynamic indicators of governance. In addition to the static attributes of accountability, responsiveness, and participation, Mehta also includes a dynamic concept of urban governance, which he calls *management innovation*. Management innovation measures the degree to which urban managers have been able to successfully implement changes in their systems of administration to achieve superior performance. Mehta introduces three measures that relate to the ability of cities to transform global opportunities to local value. These include measures of public-private partnerships, local government-citizen interaction, and networking.

A number of authors see the ability of cities to engage in public-private partnerships as a key capability for staying power in a global scene (see Doel and Hubbard 2002 and Knox 2002). Mehta suggests measures including the presence of business-sector initiatives to improve the efficiency of local government, as well as the degree to which implementation of policies and incentive schemes exist to encourage private sector participation in development. Such indicators are relevant because transnational corporations often evaluate the advantages of locating in a given city based on the quality of engagement with the local government, as well as the local investment climate they would face.

Having city governments interact with citizens and nongovernmental organizations opens up the space for introducing the global civil society in decision making at the local level. Cities with a large diaspora that is actively involved in local decisions are one example, but so are the networks of civil society that interact on a global scale with respect to local issues (Sassen 2002).

Mehta's definition of urban governance also allows us to introduce the concept of *networking* of one city with other cities, with key actors such as firms, labor unions, and business associations, and with other states. He suggests a number of indicators of networking, such as the number of intercity, regional, and international networks, as well as the extent of technological interchange and collaboration. Other measures suggested are the exchange between cities of expertise and training. The recent example of the city of Rome sending experts to Kigali to support them in shaping their city strategy, indicates the extent to which this indicator is relevant.

Urban governance as an outcome that is visible to a citizen is a key feature that allows empirical tests of the city as a place or as a sustained achievement of performances. There are very few existing indicators that can be used to capture dynamic changes in governance at the city level. We draw on measures defined by authors such as Mehta (1998) and the UNCHS (1999), which include: (a) consumer satisfaction (survey/complaints); (b) openness of procedures for contracts/tenders for municipal services; (c) percentage of population served by services; and (d) access of the public to stages of the policy cycle.[7]

With these measures, we construct a vector of urban governance indicators that we use to test the impact of urban governance on city performance. The vector consists of measures of voice and participation and transparency and accountability, which we take from the UN database. We also use measures such as illegal financing, state capture, bribery in utility services, and bribery in judiciary proceedings from the Kaufmann, Léautier, and Mastruzzi (KLM) database. Finally, we construct a dynamic indicator of city transparency, which uses proxies such as whether a city has a web page, what information is included in the web page, whether the city budget is publicly available on the web or whether companies can register on the web. Note that this indicator is similar to the one described earlier and attributed to Townsend (2001).

Defining the Impact of Urban Governance on Globalized Cities

A "globalized city" as an *enduring performance* is a concept worth testing empirically. We can ask what aspects of governance give cities this capability to constantly translate global complexities to their own advantage, which can be seen in the way they treat their citizens (access to services, quality of services), in their ability to attract firms to invest (public-private partnerships, FDI, firm location), and in their success in maintaining economic growth over several years and increasing the average per capita income of a city's citizens. Doel and Hubbard (2002) suggest that a globalized city is always a work in progress being shaped and managed by firms, states, sectors, and cities. Thus, a city that has good governance should be able to perform well, to remain in the league of important global cities, and to deliver value to its citizens.

The literature on globalization and urban governance has two schools of thought on the importance of globalization for the performance of cities. One school argues that cities can be well performing if they have sufficient spatial agglomeration of know-how and capacity in the city and that a city's international competitiveness is quite different from the concept of an international city (Kresl 1995, p. 54). Their superior performance in delivering local value to their citizens can come from their interaction with the rural hinterland, as well as with cities within the same country. Thus, well-governed cities that are not highly globalized would fit in this category, where we would expect that such cities would be well performing because they are well governed rather than because they are globalized.

The other school argues that successful cities will be those that are considered world cities and that deliver local value through interpreting and tapping into global opportunities (Doel and Hubbard 2002). Such cities attend to their own position in a global space of flows and are well governed not only in local terms but also in global terms. Their ability to remain well-performing cities in a globalized world is determined by their constant attention to good governance. De Long and Shleifer (1992) have used such a construct to look at the differential performance of cities that were ruled by princes (little voice and participation by citizens and merchants) and those ruled by merchants (more voice for citizens and firms). Because they have a long time series (from the second to the nineteenth centuries, they are able to test the relationship between good governance (measured by voice) and city performance (measured by city population and size).

Capturing the Staying Power of Cities in a Globalized World

Another important consideration is the one of scale. If scale is something produced rather than given (as pointed out by Doel and Hubbard 2002), then the size of cities is an outcome of contingent encounters between cities, firms, individuals, and sectors (business associations, labor unions, etc.). When sufficient time series data become available, it should be possible to gather "emergent governance indicators," which would allow us to look at the changes in governance over time as a result of globalization.[8] We use a function that allows us to include variables at both city- and country-level globalization as an input to delivering service performance within a city, as well as globalization as an outcome of good governance. In this manner, governance achievements provide the environment in which cities can perform better and hence tap into global opportunities.

Capturing the Dynamics of Globalization

Measures that are important to capture both the dynamics of globalization and the staying power of cities include concepts of connectivity, flow, and traffic. Those concepts can be measured by indicators defined by Doel and Hubbard (2002), such as the volume and direction of flow of people (via international migration); capital (via international banking); products (via import and export); ideas (via broadcasting and the media); pollution (via dumping policies); and even crime (drugs, human traffic, money laundering). Because these measures would change over time, the direction of change and the continuity of flows at given levels could define the staying power of cities. This definition posits the capability of cities to translate complex relationships at various levels into an advantage, and this capacity to translate is rarer than the capacity to command or control.

In its most concise definition, globalization "simply refers to the complex of forces that trend toward a single world society. Among these forces are mass communications, commerce, increased ease of travel, the internet, popular culture, and the increasingly widespread use of English as an international language" (Progressive Living 2005). Globalization has most often been analyzed at the country level. Sources of data and analysis judging country-level globalization as a dynamic concept are rare. Some authors use rankings of countries on a number of dimensions of globalization; A. T. Kearney, for example, has developed a composite index of globalization (*Foreign Policy* 2002). This index builds on indicators of trade, finance, personal contact, and information exchange. Using the Kearney database, we investigate the issue of country-level globalization and its impact on city performance, with cities judged on the ability to sustain a track record of services to their citizens.

For globalization at the city level, we utilize data from the GaWC research (Taylor and Walker 2000), which has city-level data constructed from a superposition of networks of accountancy, advertising, banking/finance, insurance, law, and management consultancy firms—the business services indicators of Friedman (1986). This database demonstrates the "unevenness of globalization" when one looks at the concentration of cities by region for example. We refer to this as the Taylor database. With such data, we can pursue the question of why some cities are left behind in globalization.

Determinants of City Performance

Because of the paucity of comparable data on cities worldwide, we need to be nimble on the model specification we use. We search for a specification that allows us to capture the dynamics of globalization, governance and performance of cities, as well as define specific hypotheses to be tested.

A Simple Framework

We specifically consider the role that governance plays at different levels of globalization of cities. We distinguish between three dimensions of globalization in Figure 3.1; two of which are inputs (quality of governance and extent of city globalization, on the vertical and horizontal axes, respectively), and one an outcome (service delivery/city performance, in the "virtual" third dimension in the chart, illustrated in the figure by the diagonal line). With such a schematic chart we define the key testable hypotheses on the effects of globalization and governance on city level performance. The hypotheses to be tested are as follows: Governance and globalization interact and do matter for city performance.

- *Hypothesis 1: Governance matters.* Can a city be well performing regardless of whether it is a local or global city, significantly driven by its good governance? And, more specifically, would a local city necessarily have to exhibit good governance to compensate and be able perform, that is, could a city be located in quadrant II and still be likely to be well performing? We posit that governance matters significantly for city performance, controlling for its level of globalization. While a local city could exceptionally exhibit good performance, this is highly unlikely unless the city exhibits relatively high levels of governance.

  Governance in this specification is an endowment that allows a city to perform well either locally or globally. In other words, we can test if a well performing city, whether local or global, has good governance, hence measuring the independent value added of governance to a local city or to a global city. The added value of governance for a local city is then the difference between the performance of a city in quadrant I compared with one in quadrant II, while the added value of governance for a global city is the differential performance of a city in quadrant IV compared with one in quadrant III.

- *Hypothesis 2: Globalization matters.* We can then also test whether a global city is better performing than a local city, for a given quality of governance (whether for a given level of good governance, as in quadrants I versus IV, or poor governance, as in quadrants II versus III, which would measure the independent effect of globalization on city performance). From the literature, it is expected that a city that is global is able to attain such global status because of specific actions taken by its political leadership or by its citizens, as well as the firms that locate within such a city. We would expect citizens of global cities to have better quality and access to services, such as water, sewerage, electricity, and telephones, than the residents of local cities.

- *Hypothesis 3: Globalization and governance interact positively.* While in principle a city could compensate for its local (versus global) character by exhibiting good governance, in practice the dynamics of good governance may point to a linkage between globalization and governance: those cities that globalize bring about the checks and balances of competition (say, by the discipline imposed by foreign direct investment and credit markets), as well as the techniques that are likely to improve city governance. In turn, improved governance, involving transparency, control of corruption, and protection of property rights, may attract further demand and pressures for a local city to become more global.[9] Thus, a dynamic virtuous circle may be at

Figure 3.1. *City Governance and Extent of Globalization as Potential Determinants of City Performance*

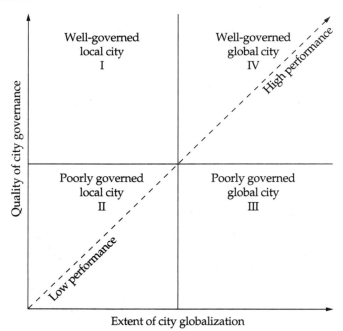

play in which globalization and governance interactive positively to further improve performance. In particular, we will empirically investigate whether good governance is less likely in local cities, and thus whether becoming a global city, and a globalized country, helps to improve city governance.

Thus, in Figure 3.1, we would expect that the worst performance would take place in cities in quadrant II (poorly governed local cities). If a city in quadrant II attempts to attain higher levels of globalization, it is unlikely to succeed without also increasing pressures to take measures to improve governance. Thus, a rapid and fully horizontal move out of quadrant II to quadrant IV or a rapid and fully vertical move to quadrant I is less likely than either the city's staying within a low equilibrium trap or moving out of quadrant II toward the good performance equilibrium in quadrant III via the diagonal route.

Simple Model Specification

A very simple model specification to analyze what emerges from these hypotheses tests is advanced as follows:

$$Y = f(X, Z, c, C) + \varepsilon$$

where

Y = city performance as measured by a vector of qualitative service variables which include access to water supply, sewerage, electricity, and telephones from the UN dataset, as well as the overall quality of infrastructure services and electricity supply, access to telephones and/or cell phones and access to internet in schools, using the EOS database.

X = measure of globalization at the city level, which we specify using the Taylor dataset as the total number of offices of major international advertising, accounting, and financial firms in a city.

Z = vector of governance indicators, which includes control of corruption, bribery in utility, and state capture, largely drawn from the EOS database.

c = other city characteristics, such as city size, whether it is the capital city, and/or a port, as well as availability of websites and availability of information on city budget and business regulations in such websites.

C = country characteristics, such as income level, size, extent of urbanization, and degree of globalization at the country level.

ε = error term.

Data Description and Mapping of Variables

The KLM database, which integrates existing data with newly collected data and indicators, covering a total of 412 cities in 134 countries, was constructed by drawing from a variety of sources. From the UN Observatory (1998), we downloaded four service access and performance variables, covering about 80 cities in 60 countries. From the enterprise-specific EOS survey database (2003), we construct city-specific averages for twelve governance indicators, as well as five service access and performance variables, covering 271 cities in 101 countries. For instance, two governance-related variables for which we constructed city-wide averages, were frequency of bribery in utility, and the extent of state capture (from firms' reports on the distortionary impact on competition of illegal payments made by certain firms) to influence government policies, laws or regulations. From the Taylor database, we downloaded the number of offices of major advertising, accounting, and financial firms in each city, and we constructed a "global city" variable by adding up the three variables, covering a total of 261 cities in 114 countries.

In addition, we also constructed indicators through internet searches, for particular city attributes, such as city population, existence of city websites, and availability of data on budget and business regulations in such websites. We completed this list of city attributes by including two dummies for whether the city is the country's capital and/or a port.

At the country level, we draw from the variable "Control of Corruption" from the Worldwide Aggregate Governance Indicators discussed above, where corruption (conventionally defined as the exercise of public power for private gain) is one of its components. The indicator is the aggregate of many individual sources, covering several aspects of corruption, ranging from administrative corruption to "grand corruption" in the political arena and "state capture." We also constructed an income per capita variable (PPP) by drawing from the Heston-Summers database and the *CIA World Factbook* (2001). For globalization at the country level, we draw from the A.T. Kearney/*Foreign Policy* Globalization Index. It tracks and assesses changes in four key components of global integration, incorporating such measures as trade and financial flows, movement of people across borders, international telephone traffic, internet usage, and participation in international treaties and peacekeeping operations. It covers 62 countries, including industrialized and emerging economies.[10] In Table 3.1 we present the legend, sources, and characteristics of all the variables we use in the empirical testing of these hypotheses.

Main Empirical Results

We performed a simple univariate or, at most, bivariate, testing of whether globalization and/or governance are highly and significantly related to city performance. In simplified chart form, we first present these results in Figures 3.2 through 3.10, which summarize the initial empirical support for the main hypotheses we tested. These figures present the results utilizing only the sample of emerging and transition economies (referred to as "non-OECD" countries), as a simple way of quasi-controlling for large income differentials (indeed, the differences are even larger with the full sample, not depicted in the figures, but shown in subsequent tables below). The figures below present the differential performance that a global (vs. local) city makes on a vector of performance in services, such as access to telephones (by the population as a whole in Figure 3.2 and by businesses in Figure 3.3),[11] sewerage (Figure 3.4), water (Figure 3.5), electricity (Figure 3.6), overall quality of infrastructure (Figure 3.7), access to cell phones (Figure 3.8), access to internet in schools (Figure 3.9), and quality of electricity supply (Figure 3.10).

Furthermore, by the simple sample segmentation and calculation performed for each of these figures, we can also depict here the difference that good governance can make. This is done utilizing three measures of governance, of which one is a country average (control of corruption), and the other two are at the city level (bribery in utility and state capture).

We find that governance is significantly associated with performance, both for local and global cities. Well-governed cities, whether local or global, perform better than poorly governed ones across all quality and access to service variables. The performance advantage of well-governed cities holds across all three measures of governance and all service variables except access to the electricity grid in global cities.

Globalization has a more nuanced effect on city performance. We find that on balance global cities do perform better than local cities. However, the differences are not that marked, and they vary depending on the type of service. In particular, the difference between local and global cities is clear for certain services, such as quality of infrastructure, yet nonexistent for access to electricity, for instance. The rest of the services rate lies in between such extremes both in terms of magnitude of its impact (often modest) as well as varying levels of significance.

We present the fuller set of average rating results for all relevant variables for each one of the relevant samples (full sample in Table 3.2, non-OECD in Table 3.3, and OECD in Table 3.4). We can clearly detect a strong positive correlation between city performance as measured by service access and the extent of globalization (both at city and country level), regardless of sample. Similarly, there appears to be a strong positive correlation between city performance/service access and governance at the city and country levels. In conclusion, more globalized cities are better performing, and better governed cities are well performing. Cities in well-governed countries are also better performing.

The significance of the link between governance and city performance is also summarized in Table 3.5 below, which presents both the magnitude (numerical) and significance (indicated by the number of asterisks) of the coefficient of a regression of service performance on governance. As we see in the table, governance is an important correlate of performance in the full sample, as well as in the subgroups of local and global cities. We note that the results are large and significant for both local and global cities (with very rare exceptions), further supporting the results illustrated in Figures 3.2–3.10 and Tables 3.2–3.4.[12]

Table 3.1. *Description and Coverage of Variables in the Kaufmann-Léautier-Mastruzzi Database*

Variable	Description/source	Range/direction	Country	City
City variables				
Access to water	UNCHS 1998	% of population	61	83
Access to sewerage	UNCHS 1998	% of population	57	78
Access to electricity	UNCHS 1998	% of population	61	81
Access to telephone lines 1	UNCHS 1998	% of population	51	58
Access to telephone lines 2	World Bank 2003	1 (bad)–7 (good)	101	271
Quality of infrastructure	World Bank 2003	1 (bad)–7 (good)	101	271
Quality of electricity	World Bank 2003	1 (bad)–7 (good)	101	271
Access to cell phones	World Bank 2003	1 (bad)–7 (good)	101	271
Access to internet in schools	World Bank 2003	1 (bad)–7 (good)	101	271
Bribery in utility	World Bank 2003	1 (bad)–7 (good)	101	271
State capture	World Bank 2003	1 (bad)–7 (good)	101	271
Informal money laundering	World Bank 2003	1 (bad)–7 (good)	101	271
Street crime	World Bank 2003	1 (bad)–7 (good)	101	271
Red tape cost of imports	World Bank 2003	1 (good)–9 (bad)	101	271
Bribery to affect laws	World Bank 2003	1 (bad)–7 (good)	101	271
Diversion of public funds	World Bank 2003	1 (bad)–7 (good)	101	271
Illegal party financing	World Bank 2003	1 (bad)–7 (good)	101	271
Bribery in permits	World Bank 2003	1 (bad)–7 (good)	101	271
Bribery in tax	World Bank 2003	1 (bad)–7 (good)	101	271
Soundness of banks	World Bank 2003	1 (bad)–7 (good)	101	271
Trust in politicians	World Bank 2003	1 (bad)–7 (good)	101	271
Organized crime	World Bank 2003	1 (bad)–7 (good)	101	271
Quality of postal system	World Bank 2003	1 (bad)–7 (good)	101	271
Health access gap	World Bank 2003	1 (bad)–7 (good)	101	271
Global city	Number of offices of major advertising, financial, and accounting firms taken from Taylor and Walker 2001	Hundreds	114	261
City population	www.citypopulation.de.2001	Logs	134	410
Website dummy	City has a website (Kaufmann, Léautier, and Mastruzzi 2003)	0 (no)–1 (yes)	133	398
Business dummy	City website has information on how to start a business (Kaufmann, Léautier, and Mastruzzi 2003)	0 (no)–1 (yes)	133	398
Budget dummy	City website has information on budget (Kaufmann, Léautier, and Mastruzzi 2003)	0 (no)–1 (yes)	133	398
Port dummy	City has port facilities (Kaufmann, Léautier, and Mastruzzi 2003)	0 (no)–1 (yes)	134	411
Capital city dummy	City is the capital (Kaufmann, Léautier, and Mastruzzi 2003)	0 (no)–1 (yes)	134	411
Country variables				
Globalization index (Kearney)	*Foreign Policy* 2002	0 (closed)–1 (open)	59	254
Control of corruption	Governance indicator (Kaufmann and Kraay 2002)	–2.5 (bad)– +2.5 (good)	134	411
Country population	World Bank 2002	Logs	134	411
Urbanization	% of population not in agriculture (World Bank 2002)	% of population	100	366
Income per capita	Summers and Heston 1984; CIA 2001	Logs	134	411

Figure 3.2. *City Performance on Access of the Population to Telephones by Levels of Globalization and Governance in the Non-OECD Sample*

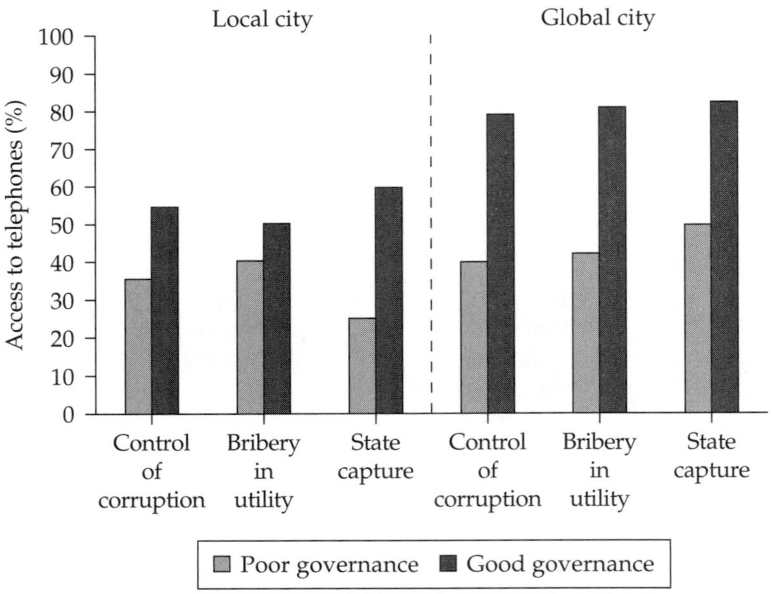

Note: Access of the population to telephones is drawn from UN Observatory 1998 and measures the percentage of the population with access to telephones.
    Sources: World Bank 2003; UNCHS 1998; Kaufmann and Kraay 2002; and Kaufmann, Léautier, and Mastruzzi 2003.

Figure 3.3. *City Performance on Access of Businesses to Telephones by Levels of Globalization and Governance in the Non-OECD Sample*

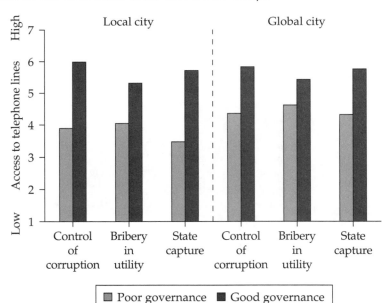

Note: Access of businesses to telephones is drawn from EOS 2003 and captures on a scale of 1-7 the availability of new telephone lines for business.
    Sources: World Bank 2003; Kaufmann and Kraay 2002; and Kaufmann, Léautier, and Mastruzzi 2003.

Figure 3.4. *City Performance on Access to Sewerage by Levels of Globalization and Governance in the Non-OECD Sample*

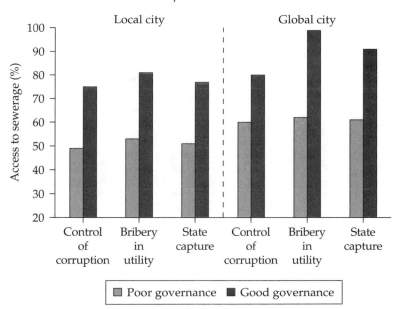

Sources: World Bank 2003; UNCHS 1998; Kaufmann and Kraay 2002; and Kaufmann, Léautier, and Mastruzzi 2003.

Figure 3.5. *City Performance on Access to Water by Levels of Globalization and Governance in the Non-OECD Sample*

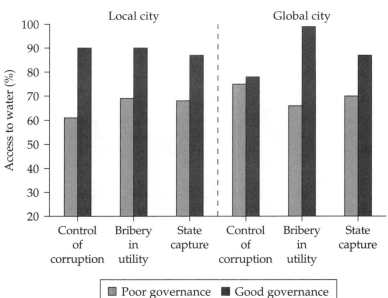

Sources: World Bank 2003; UNCHS 1998; Kaufmann and Kraay 2002; and Kaufmann, Léautier, and Mastruzzi 2003.

Figure 3.6. *City Performance on Access to Electricity by Levels of Globalization and Governance in the Non-OECD Sample*

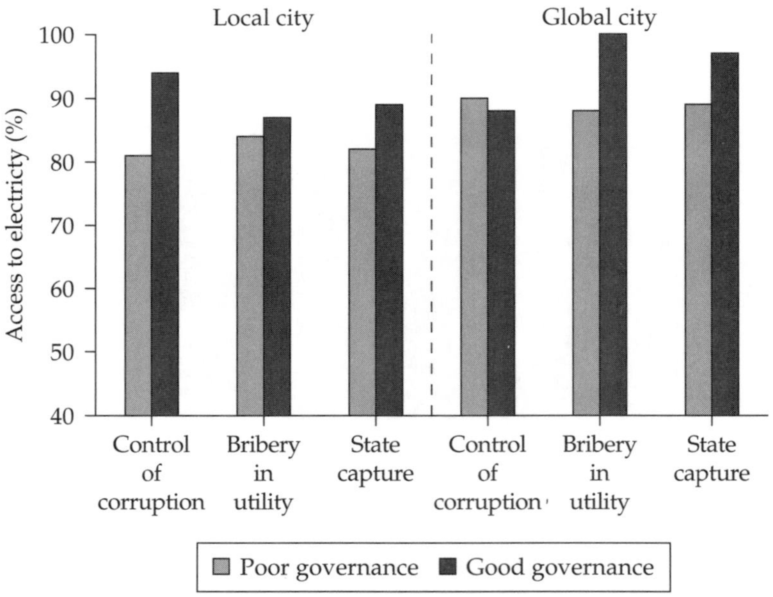

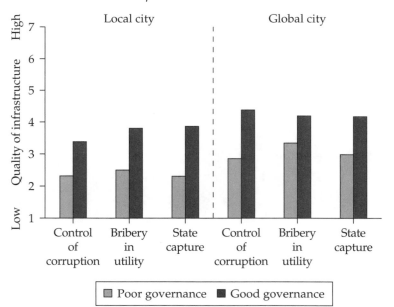

Sources: World Bank 2003; UNCHS 1998; Kaufmann and Kraay 2002; and Kaufmann, Léautier, and Mastruzzi 2003.

Figure 3.7. *City Performance on Quality of Infrastructure by Levels of Globalization and Governance in the Non-OECD Sample*

Sources: World Bank 2003; UNCHS 1998; Kaufmann and Kraay 2002; and Kaufmann, Léautier, and Mastruzzi 2003.

Figure 3.8. *City Performance on Access to Cell Phones by Levels of Globalization and Governance in the Non-OECD Sample*

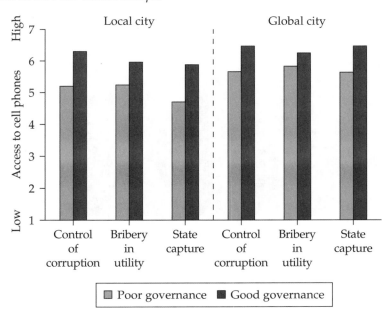

Sources: World Bank 2003; UNCHS 1998; Kaufmann and Kraay 2002; and Kaufmann, Léautier, and Mastruzzi 2003.

Figure 3.9. *City Performance on Access to Internet in Schools by Levels of Globalization and Governance in the Non-OECD Sample*

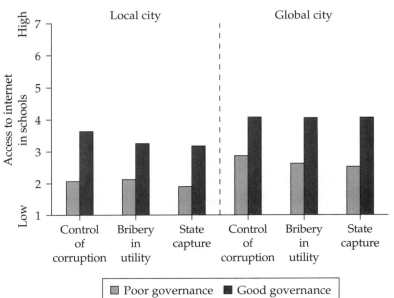

Sources: World Bank 2003; UNCHS 1998; Kaufmann and Kraay 2002; and Kaufmann, Léautier, and Mastruzzi 2003.

***Figure* 3.10.** *City Performance on Quality of Electricity by Levels of Globalization and Governance in the Non-OECD Sample*

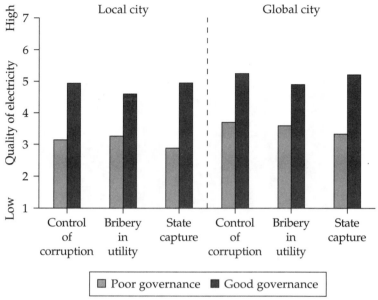

Sources: EOS 2003; Kaufmann and Kraay 2002; and Kaufmann, Léautier, and Mastruzzi 2003.

***Table* 3.2.** *City Performance by Levels of Globalization and Governance in the Full Sample*

| | Globalization measures | | | | Governance measures | | | | | |
| | City globalization | | Country globalization | | Bribery in utility | | State capture | | Country control of corruption | |
Variable	Low	High	Low	High	Poor	Good	Poor	Good	Poor	Good
Access to sewerage (%, UN)	62	94	75	99	55	91	60	89	62	95
Access to water (%, UN)	75	95	81	100	68	96	72	94	73	98
Access to electricity %, UN)	90	94	90	100	82	95	83	95	85	100
Access to telephones 1 (%, UN)	46	80	60	95	37	79	41	80	40	89
Access to telephones 2 (1–7, EOS)	4.8	6.0	5.4	6.4	4.4	6.2	4.6	6.0	4.6	6.2
Access to cellular phones (1–7, EOS)	5.7	6.5	6.1	6.7	5.5	6.5	5.6	6.4	5.6	6.5
Access to internet in schools (1–7, EOS)	2.9	4.7	3.7	5.3	2.9	4.8	3.0	4.7	2.9	5.0
Quality of infrastructure (1–7, EOS)	3.1	5.0	3.5	5.5	2.9	4.7	2.9	4.7	2.9	5.0
Quality of electricity (1–7, EOS)	3.9	5.6	4.4	6.2	3.6	5.7	3.8	5.4	3.7	5.8
Overall number of cities	132	129	131	123	137	134	136	135	211	201

Note: The full sample comprises 412 cities. Each column variable was segmented into two equal samples, below and above the median value of the full sample.

Source: UN Urban Observatory 1998; World Bank 2003; Taylor and Walker 2001; *Foreign Policy* 2002; Kaufmann and Kraay 2002.

Table 3.3. *City Performance by Levels of Globalization and Governance in the Non-OECD Sample*

| | Globalization measures | | | | Governance measures | | | | | |
| | City globalization | | Country globalization | | Bribery in utility | | State capture | | Country control of corruption | |
Variable	Low	High	Low	High	Poor	Good	Poor	Good	Poor	Good
Access to sewerage (%, UN)	57	72	71	79	50	87	51	82	56	72
Access to water (%, UN)	74	79	78	85	64	93	66	88	70	81
Access to electricity (%, UN)	87	90	88	92	80	93	80	92	83	90
Access to telephones 1 (%, UN)	43	57	48	76	32	74	38	64	37	59
Access to telephones 2 (1–7, EOS)	4.4	5.1	5.4	5.4	4.2	5.6	4.4	5.4	4.1	5.6
Access to cellular phones (1–7, EOS)	5.4	6.1	6.2	6.1	5.4	6.2	5.5	6.0	5.4	6.1
Access to internet in schools (1-7, EOS)	2.4	3.3	3.5	3.9	2.7	4.0	2.8	3.9	2.6	4.1
Quality of infrastructure (1–7, EOS)	2.6	3.7	3.5	3.4	2.8	3.8	2.7	3.9	2.7	3.8
Quality of electricity (1–7, EOS)	3.6	4.4	4.2	4.5	3.4	4.8	3.6	4.6	3.4	4.8
Overall number of cities	70	65	61	61	102	102	106	98	138	136

Note: The non-OECD sample comprises 274 cities. Each column variable was segmented into two equal samples, below and above the median value of the full sample.

Source: UNCHS 1998; World Bank 2003; Taylor and Walker 2001; *Foreign Policy* 2002; Kaufmann and Kraay 2002.

The results also suggest that these substantial additional benefits of improving governance generally do not differ significantly depending on whether the city is globally or locally oriented (as indicated in the table by small magnitudes and lack of significance of the "difference" row for each service). The exception is the case of control of corruption and access to water and to telephones, which seem more important for local cities than global cities; and bribery in utility, quality of infrastructure, and access to internet at schools, which are more important for global cities. These results may hint at the possibility of differential weights on the type of service that matters for local versus global cities. The results for sewerage are also quite high and could be due to other efforts. More details on the technological and network aspects of services can be found in the section, Determinants of City Governance.

We broaden our presentation of the statistical results by summarizing the evidence obtained from the multivariate econometric specifications, where a fuller set of controls in multiple specifications explaining service performance was included. As with the description of the simple model and the variables presented in the previous section, we performed econometric tests through ordinary least squares specifications with the various service performance outcomes as dependent variables and with the city characteristics, city and country governance, globalization indicators, and country characteristics as independent variables.

Table 3.6 presents the combined synthesis of the results of all econometric specifications. This synthesis presents the magnitude values (with +, 0, or - on the left)

Table 3.4. *City Performance by Levels of Globalization and Governance in the OECD Sample*

	Globalization measures				Governance measures					
	City globalization		Country globalization		Bribery in utility		State capture		Country control of corruption	
Variable	Low	High	Low	High	Poor	Good	Poor	Good	Poor	Good
Access to sewerage (%, UN)	98	100	99	100	98	100	98	100	99	100
Access to water (%, UN)	99	100	100	100	100	100	100	100	99	100
Access to electricity (%, UN)	100	100	100	100	100	100	100	100	100	100
Access to telephones 1 (%, UN)	92	96	92	99	93	100	93	99	92	99
Access to telephones 2 (1-7, EOS)	5.9	6.6	6.2	6.7	6.2	6.8	6.2	6.7	6.0	6.8
Access to cellular phones (1-7, EOS)	6.5	6.7	6.5	6.8	6.5	6.8	6.5	6.8	6.4	6.8
Access to internet in schools (1-7, EOS)	4.8	5.4	4.8	5.9	5.0	5.6	4.8	5.8	4.5	5.9
Quality of infrastructure (1-7, EOS)	4.8	5.7	5.1	5.9	4.9	6.1	4.9	6.0	4.6	6.1
Quality of electricity (1-7, EOS)	5.5	6.3	5.8	6.6	5.8	6.6	5.7	6.7	5.6	6.6
Overall number of cities	64	62	90	42	34	33	34	33	73	65

Note: The OECD sample comprises 138 cities. Each column variable was segmented into two equal samples, below and above the median value of the full sample.

Source: UNCHS 1998; World Bank 2003; Taylor and Walker 2001; *Foreign Policy* 2002; Kaufmann and Kraay 2002.

and significance (with asterisks on the right), which we obtain by averaging the magnitude and significance of the regression results of 21 different ordinary least squares specifications for each city performance indicator.[13]

From the implementation of the fuller econometric model, we obtain a number of salient results. There is an effect of the variable city globalization on performance using both the Taylor (global city variable) and the UN (water, electricity, telephone, and sewerage access variables) databases. This effect is relatively modest in some cases yet present, though with varying levels of significance depending on the type of service, controls used, and model specifications. The variable that is most correlated to city globalization (global city 3) is the quality of electricity.

Other city globalization proxies, such as whether the city has a web portal with information on steps to start a firm (business dummy) and whether the budget is transparently available on the web (budget dummy), show positive and significant results, but these results are not robust across all service variables. In particular, access to cell phones (as opposed to telephones), and the overall quality of infrastructure are significant, while the other service variables, such as access to water, electricity, and sewerage, and to telephone lines show less significance. See the section, Determinants of City Governance, for a more detailed treatment of some of the city characteristics and related results. Bribery in utility seems to also be important, showing significant results for all service variables in Table 3.6.

The definition of city as a space is sensitive to the definitions of city boundaries, whether core city or broader agglomeration. We have corrected for this by using the

Table 3.5. *City Performance and Service Access by Level of Governance for Global and Local Cities*

Performance variable and sample	Bribery in utility	State capture	Control of corruption
Access to water			
Full city sample	0.11***	0.10***	0.11***
Global city sample	0.10*	0.04	0.06*
Local city sample	0.09**	0.10**	0.15***
Differential	0.01	−0.06	−0.09*
Access to sewerage			
Full city sample	0.15***	0.13***	0.16***
Global city sample	0.13	0.07	0.08*
Local city sample	0.13**	0.11	0.21**
Differential	0.00	−0.04	−0.13
Access to electricity			
Full city sample	0.05**	0.05**	0.05***
Global city sample	0.05	0.06*	0.06**
Local city sample	0.05*	0.07*	0.07**
Differential	0.00	−0.01	−0.01
Access to telephones (1)			
Full city sample	0.19***	0.15***	0.24***
Global city sample	0.17***	0.13**	0.14***
Local city sample	0.16***	0.09	0.32***
Differential	0.01	0.04	−0.18
Quality of infrastructure			
Full city sample	0.99***	0.98***	1.10***
Global city sample	0.96***	0.86***	0.99***
Local city sample	0.57***	0.82***	0.87***
Differential	0.39***	0.04	0.12
Quality of electricity			
Full city sample	1.06***	0.92***	1.10***
Global city sample	1.05***	0.82***	0.99***
Local city sample	0.80***	0.79***	0.87***
Differential	0.25	0.03	0.12
Access to telephones (2)			
Full city sample	0.87***	0.85***	0.82***
Global city sample	0.81***	0.53***	0.70***
Local city sample	0.92***	0.78***	1.10***
Differential	-0.11	-0.25	-0.40
Access to cell phones			
Full city sample	0.43***	0.35***	0.44***
Global city sample	0.39***	0.30***	0.34***
Local city sample	0.35***	0.21*	0.53***
Differential	0.04	0.09	-0.19
Internet access at achool			
Full city sample	0.99***	0.93***	1.12***
Global city sample	0.97***	0.82***	0.98***
Local city sample	0.64***	0.78***	1.21***
Differential	0.34*	0.04	-0.23

Note: Initial sample of 262 cities was divided into two equal samples according to whether the city is global or local. We then ran a set of univariate pooled regressions of service performance and access variables against selected governance variables (bribery in utility, state capture, and control of corruption. The results for the magnitude and significance of coefficients for global and local samples are reported in the global city and local city rows, respectively. In each econometric specification we also included a dummy (for global city = 1, and local city = 0) to identify the two samples, as well as an interactive term (dummy = governance) to capture the differential impact of governance on city performance between global and local cities. Differential indicates the differential of the coefficients, along with the coefficients on governance variables for full sample and subsets. Refer also to Annex 3.1 for the correlation matrix.

Table 3.6. *Synthesis of Econometric Regression Results on Determinants of City Performance*

Dependent variables	Access to water	Access to electricity	Access to sewerage	Access to telephones (1)	Access to telephones (2)	Access to cell phones	Internet access	Quality of infrastructure	Quality of electricity
City variables									
City population	0/0	0/0	0/0	0/0	+/0	+/0	0/0	+/*	+/0
Global city (3)	0/0	0/0	0/0	0/0	+/0	0/0	0/0	+/0	+/**
Bribery in utility	+/'	0/'	+/'	+/*	+++/***	++/***	-/0	++++/***	++++/***
Business dummy	0/0	0/0	0/0	+/'	+/'	0/*	0/0	+++/**	++/**
Website dummy	0/0	0/'	0/0	+/0	++/**	+/**	0/0	+/*	+/'
Budget dummy	0/'	0/0	0/*	0/0	+/*	0/0	+/0	+/0	0/0
Port dummy	-/**	0/'	0/0	-/**	+/0	0/0	+/*	0/**	-/*
Capital dummy	0/0	0/0	0/0	0/0	-/0	-/0	+/***	-/*	0/0
Country variables									
Country population	0/0	0/0	0/0	0/0	0/0	0/0	++/**	0/0	-/*
Urbanization	+/'	0/'	0/0	+/'	+/0	+/0	0/*	0/'	+/'
Kearney globalization Index	0/'	0/0	0/0	+/0	+/*	+/*	+/*	+++/***	+++/***
Control of corruption	+/**	0/*	+/'	+/**	++++/***	++/**	+/0	++++/***	++++/***
Income per capita	+/***	+/**	++/***	++/***	++++/***	+++/***	+++/***	++++/***	++++/***
Number of cities	63	61	59	42	194	194	194	194	194
Adjusted R^2	0.28	0.11	0.29	0.37	0.39	0.28	0.28	0.45	0.50

Note: The sample includes 412 cities in 134 countries. Values for magnitude (+, 0, -) and significance (*, 0, ') in each cell were obtained by averaging results of 21 different ordinary least squares specifications. In particular, for each independent variable, for calculating the magnitude of the coefficient rating (left-hand side), we computed the product of the average coefficient magnitude across all specifications times twice the standard deviation of the variable. Then we assigned magnitude values according to the following criteria: for positive coefficients, we applied a "++++" for any value above 1.2, "+++" for any value between 0.7 and 1.2, "++" for any value between 0.4 and 0.7, "+" for any value between 0.1 and 0.4, and finally a "0" for any value below 0.1. Similarly, minus signs were applied to negative coefficients. For the rating on the significance of the coefficient in each cell (right hand side), we averaged the various significance levels across the 21 specifications, where *** indicates significance at 1 percent, ** indicates significance at 5 percent, * indicates significance at 10 percent and ' indicates significance at 15 percent. Values for number of cities and R^2 were computed as simple averages across all specifications.

Source: All dependent variables drawn from UNCHS 1998 and World Bank 2003; globalization index downloaded from Foreign Policy 2002; country population and urbanization drawn from World Bank 2002, city population downloaded from website: www.citypopulation.de; port, capital, budget and business dummies drawn from Kaufmann, Léautier, and Mastruzzi 2003; control of corruption drawn from Kaufmann and Kraay 2002; Global city (3) drawn from Taylor and Walker 2001; income per capita drawn from Summers and Heston (1984) and *World Factbook* (CIA 2001); bribery in utility drawn from World Bank 2003.

definition of city as an outcome for the analysis. Such a construct: (a) allows us to use "city as a place" as an input to the analysis and hence is less sensitive to the boundary definitions; and (b) the UN database has data on city size by core city and urban agglomeration, and we did not find any differences when either of the two measures were used. In any case, the data have measurement errors, as does any database, and thus we used similar indicators from different sources (for example, access to telephones in UN databases and the same indicator in EOS database) to check the sensitivity of the results across databases. These results are robust and independent of the definition of city boundaries. We did control for various definitions of city boundaries by running regressions both on core city population and metropolitan population, with same results.

These econometric results are consistent with and support what was described in the previous figures and tables. Indeed, the results suggest that there are differential impacts of globalization on city performance, depending on the options city residents have for exit or choice. In the services where they can exit, such as water and electricity, then globalization has limited impact on city performance. In cases where they cannot exit, globalization seems to have more impact, and the role of voice and participation are critical, as shown by the significance of the variables for bribery in utility and control of corruption.

Lee and Anas (1996) potently gave an illustration consistent with these results. They analyzed the decisions firms made to locate or not in cities in Nigeria and Indonesia, and they found that, where public supply of electricity was unreliable, the firms could substitute by private generation capacity that they themselves installed. Chapter 6 provides a more detailed look at both the issue of technology and that of scale and city characteristics.

Country globalization (as indicated by the Kearney Globalization Index) also matters for city-level performance. It is significant for all service variables except access to electricity, sewerage, and telephone lines. What is interesting in the results in Table 3.6 is that city performance for network infrastructure (electricity grid, sewerage, telephone lines) is impacted by two aspects of governance (bribery in utility at the city level, control of corruption at the country level) and per capita income. Rich countries can afford to provide network infrastructure in cities. And better control of city- and country-level corruption leads to better performance of cities in providing access to services.

In summary, we find that there is an effect of city globalization on the performance of cities using both the Taylor and the UN databases. While the strength of the effect appears to be somewhat more robust for governance variables, it is also present for globalization variables.

Determinants of City Governance

The dramatic increase in empirical work on governance over the past few years has led to a more in-depth analysis of the manifestations, causes, and consequences of misgovernance and corruption. It has drawn from cross-country data as well as in-country diagnostic perspectives. Significant inroads have been made in unbundling governance to measure and analyze its detailed components, as well as in exploring empirically the governance performance of different institutions such as parliament, police, and customs.

A Simple Framework

We use three indicators of governance to investigate the relationship between globalization and governance. The first is an indicator of governance from the political perspective, which we represent by an indicator of low illegal party financing. The second is a measure of public sector governance for which we use an indicator on low diversion of public funds. Third, we use an indicator of the effectiveness of public services where we use a measure of trust and performance of the postal system. With these three indicators, we see that globalization is positively related to good governance (Figure 3.11).

For city governance we use a measure of whether a city is providing services to its citizens (low health access gap) and whether it has a well functioning public sector with low bribery in taxes or in the provision of utilities. The data shows that, the more urbanized a country is, the better its level of city governance (Figure 3.12). This finding is of historical importance as most of what we now practice in the form of country governance was first developed in ancient Greece or Jericho thousands of years ago. As illustrated in Figure 3.13, the data suggest that neither city nor country size negatively affect governance at the city level. Furthermore, there is no evidence that a higher degree of urbanization within a country has a detrimental impact on the governance of cities; in fact, for some dimensions the extent of urbanization may have a positive effect.

We find no support for the argument that capital cities are better or worse governed than other cities. This finding contrasts with the empirical importance of the extent of globalization, if we assume that capital cities tend to be more globalized (Figure 3.13).

Figure 3.11. City Governance and Globalization

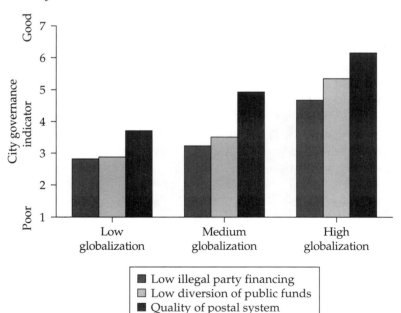

Source: World Economic Forum 2003.

Figure 3.12. *City Governance and Urbanization*

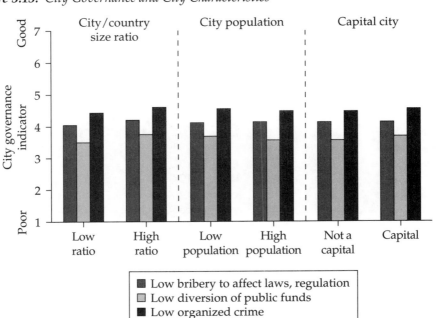

Source: World Economic Forum 2003.

Figure 3.13. *City Governance and City Characteristics*

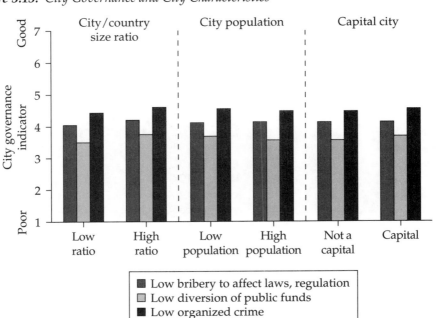

Source: World Economic Forum 2003.

This early exploration suggests that some commonly held beliefs on city-level performance can be empirically challenged-such as the notions that in larger cities performance and governance will suffer because of diseconomies of agglomeration; that port cities, or the country's capital, will generally tend to be more corrupt than other cities; or that urbanization or globalization may bring about poor governance. We summarize in Table 3.7 the key average ratings for the governance variables we utilize, against the various potential determinants.

Next, we review whether the results we have found are robust across databases and across different definitions of globalization and governance. The results are shown in Table 3.7 below. Overall, we observe higher levels of governance in global cities, although the magnitude of the differences between local and global cities varies depending on the type of governance variable used. These results are similar for the full sample of 412 cities (shown in Table 3.7) and for the samples segmented into non-OECD and OECD cities (not shown).

We find that globalization at both city and country level (Kearney Globalization Index) is positively correlated with all the measures of governance. Globalization at the country level, as measured by the Kearney Globalization Index, is significant and positive against all the governance indicators, except cost of imports where it is significant and negative. Per capita income is also positively correlated with all dimensions of governance.

These results, shown in Table 3.8, are relatively robust and significant. With some specifications, country-level globalization seems to dominate the city globalization variable. This dominance may be partly because globalization in the more fundamental (macroeconomic and trade) sense is even more important at the country level than city-specific measures. Yet, this result may also reflect the fact that the

Table 3.7. *Average Governance Ratings by City and Country Characteristics*

Dependent variable	Sample	Low bribery in utility	Low informal money laundering	Low street crime	Red tape cost of imports	Low bribery to affect laws	Low illegal party financing	Low diversion of public funds
Global city	Local	4.39	3.46	3.78	23.8	3.61	3.14	3.06
(Taylor)	Global	5.64	4.46	4.84	14.2	4.76	3.93	4.42
Size ratio	Local	4.95	3.72	4.27	17.4	3.99	3.33	3.44
city/country	Global	5.05	4.00	4.32	18.2	4.24	3.53	3.76
City population	Local	5.06	3.85	4.32	16.4	4.11	3.46	3.66
	Global	4.94	3.92	4.27	19.7	4.17	3.43	3.59
Capital city	Local	5.01	3.85	4.26	17.2	4.14	3.45	3.63
	Global	4.99	3.92	4.33	19.2	4.11	3.42	3.60
Website has info on how to start a business	Local	4.90	3.76	4.16	18.5	4.04	3.37	3.50
	Global	6.19	5.19`	5.42	10.7	5.18	4.26	5.02
Globalization	Local	4.69	3.58	4.00	20.6	3.90	3.03	3.16
(Kearney)	Global	6.21	4.88	5.46	9.6	5.11	4.36	5.04
Urbanization	Local	4.40	3.58	3.93	21.5	3.65	3.12	3.10
	Global	5.84	4.26	4.77	13.0	4.79	3.88	4.34

Note: All variables in columns range from 1 (bad) to 7 (good), with the exception of the cost of imports, which is shown in percentage terms.
Source: World Bank 2003.

Table 3.8. *Synthesis of Econometric Regression Results on Determinants of City Governance*

Dependent variables	Low bribery in utilities	Low informal money laundering	Low street crime	Red tape cost of imports	Low bribery to affect laws	Low diversion of public funds	Low illegal party financing
City variables							
City population	+/'	+/'	0/0	0/0	+/0	+/'	0/0
Global city (3)	+/'	++/***	+/'	-/**	++/**	++/**	++/***
Country/city size ratio	+/'	+/'	+/'	0/0	+/'	+/'	+/*
Business dummy	++/***	+++/***	++/**	-/'	++/**	+++/***	++/**
Website dummy	+/0	+/'	+/0	0/0	+/0	+/'	0/0
Budget dummy	0/0	+/0	+/0	0/0	-/0	0/0	0/0
Port dummy	0/0	+/'	+/0	0/0	0/0	+/'	+/'
Capital dummy	0/0	-/'	0/0	+/0	-/0	-/'	-/'
Country variables							
Country population	-/***	-/'	-/0	++/'	-/*	-/'	-/**
Urbanization	++/**	0/0	-/'	0/'	+/'	0/0	0/0
Kearney Globalization Index	++++/***	++++/***	++++/***	-/***	+++/***	++++/***	++++/***
Income per capita	++++/***	+++/***	++++/***	-/***	++++/***	++++/***	+++/***
Number of cities	193	193	193	193	193	193	193
Adjusted R^2	0.30	0.21	0.19	0.24	0.21	0.29	0.17

Note: The sample includes 412 cities in 134 countries. Values for magnitude (+, 0, -) and significance (*, 0, ') in each cell were obtained by averaging results of 21 different ordinary least squares specifications. In particular, for each independent variable, for calculating the magnitude of the coefficient rating (left-hand side), we computed the product of the average coefficient magnitude across all specifications times twice the standard deviation of the variable. Then we assigned magnitude values according to the following criteria: for positive coefficients, we applied a "++++" for any value above 1.2, "+++" for any value between 0.7 and 1.2, "++" for any value between 0.4 and 0.7, "+" for any value between 0.1 and 0.4, and finally a "0" for any value below 0.1. Similarly, minus signs were applied to negative coefficients. For the rating on the significance of the coefficient in each cell (right hand side), we averaged the various significance levels across the 21 specifications, where *** indicates significance at 1 percent, ** indicates significance at 5 percent, * indicates significance at 10 percent and ' indicates significance at 15 percent. Values for number of cities and R^2 were computed as simple averages across all specifications.

Source: All dependent variables drawn from UNCHS 1998 and World Bank 2003; globalization index downloaded from Foreign Policy 2002; country population and urbanization drawn from World Bank 2002, city population downloaded from website: www.citypopulation.de; port, capital, budget and business dummies drawn from Kaufmann, Léautier, and Mastruzzi 2003; control of corruption drawn from Kaufmann and Kraay 2002; Global city (3) drawn from Taylor and Walker 2001; income per capita drawn from Summers and Heston (1984) and *World Factbook* (CIA 2001); bribery in utility drawn from World Bank 2003.

country globalization variable was constructed specifically to have a globalization indicator, while the city globalization variables we are utilizing are indirect (and partial) proxies. Thus, the measurement errors may differ, with the city variables being more statistically "noisy."

Two proxies for city-level globalization look at cities that have attracted business in finance, accounting, and advertising (global city 3) and those that have a transparent way of allowing firms to set up a business (business dummies). In both cases, cities that are more global are better governed in all dimensions of governance.

We have summarized the results of the many econometric specifications to explain the potential determinants of city governance in the synthesis in Table 3.8. (The full set of regressions is available upon request).[14]

Future Research and Emerging Policy Implications

In this chapter we attempted to contribute to the field of urban governance and globalization through an empirically-based exploration of some key determinants of the performance of cities. This empirical inquiry was made possible through the construction of a worldwide database for cities that contains variables and indicators of globalization (at the country and city level), of city governance, and of city performance (access and quality of infrastructure service delivery). This city database integrates existing data with new data gathered specifically for this research project. We found that good governance and globalization matter for city-level performance in the access to infrastructure services and the quality of their delivery. We also found that globalization and good city governance are related. There appear to be dynamic pressures from globalization and accountability that result in better performance at the city level. Furthermore, we found complex interactions among technology, governance, and city performance, as well as evidence of a non-linear (∪-shaped) relationship between city size and performance, challenging the view that very large cities necessarily exhibit lower performance and pointing to potential agglomeration economies. Our framework also suggests a way of bridging two seemingly competing strands of the literature, namely, viewing the city as a *place* or as an *outcome*. We find evidence that port cities seem to be in general more dependent on good governance for the city performance variables that matter for globalization (access to cell phones, internet access) and that capital cities tend to serve local sewerage access better (water, sewerage, electricity).

A preliminary analysis of city level data from EOS 2004 corroborates the main findings in our chapter (summarized in Annexes 3.1 and 3.2). These results were corroborated by replacing 2003 data with 2004 data. Finally, 2004 data confirm the strong positive correlation between city performance and globalization, as well as the strong positive correlation between city performance and city governance that we found above. This indicates the robustness of our results.

Issues for Future Research

There are a number of issues to consider for future research. With our dataset and empirical approach, we encountered statistical limits after crossing variables from different datasets (Taylor, UN, and EOS) in terms of the overlapping number of observations, which for some indicators resulted in a very small number of cities being covered. Thus, a major challenge in the next stage is to expand this database and fill in the significant gaps within the existing set of over 400 cities. We expect to be able to collaborate with partners in this initiative. This expanded database would be made available on the web to all researchers and policy makers (see Annex 3.3 for the current list of cities for which this dataset has information on at least some of the variables of interest in this research project).

We also need to probe much deeper than was possible in this preliminary exploration on the dynamics between globalization and governance and their interface with city performance. For instance, we found that globalization and governance are positively correlated with each other at the city level. Our simple conceptual and econometric model pointed to possible causality from globalization to good governance. Yet, it cannot be ruled out that the causality runs both ways, within an endogenous model where there is a possible virtuous circle between both variables. Within such a framework, an extension of the simple model presented in this chapter would be warranted.[15] This requires further research with additional data and a more complex econometric model with instruments accounting for endogeneity issues, among others. Furthermore, in this context the brief references to ancient times made earlier suggest the need to probe further with an historical perspective. We continue this line of investigation in Chapter 5 in this volume.

Given the constraints in data availability at the city and country level, in this initial research inquiry we did not include some other important institutional dimensions, such as decentralization and local finance. Obviously, it cannot be ruled out that some of the significance of the governance variables for which we did have measures at the city and country level, such as the corruption-related ones, may be picking up in part some of the importance of other governance and institutional variables. Future research would need to delve more deeply into these issues of potential omitted variable biases and expand the database to account for additional institutional variables at the city level. Similarly, in future research it will be desirable to include proxies for economic output or productivity at the city level. There is a limited database for city product per capita by the UN, which suitably expanded and updated, could be used, for instance. Simple plotgrams with these limited dataset suggest that city product does improve with globalization (see Chapter 4 in this volume).[16]

Policy Implications

First, our results suggest that reforms should focus on improving national governance, which can not only help to increase economic benefits for the country at large but also provide a stronger platform for cities to improve their own procedural transparency and public participation. Furthermore, international financial institutions, such as the World Bank, and donors ought to continue to monitor and assess the quality of national governance in their member or partner countries. This makes sense not only as a means of improving countrywide performance, but also to point to ways of improving city-level performance.

Second, our framework and evidence also points to the fact that improving governance at the city level allows cities to translate global opportunity into local value for their citizens. This implies that reformist city leaders have important local policy and institutional levers at their disposal: governance at the local level matters significantly for urban performance. Similarly, this finding suggests that donor agencies could focus more on supporting improvements in city-level governance.

Finally, our findings should encourage institutions and donors to work with city governments and intercity networks and partnerships to support their globalization efforts, especially through the use of web technologies. In practical terms, cities and local networks can benefit from web-related information outreach innovations, such as placing procurement information and the budget on the city website, as well as a one-stop information and licensing 'e-window' for business start-ups. In this context, it may also be important to have a set of incentives and strategies for cities to network with other cities to tap into global opportunities that will benefit a given city.[17]

Annex 3.1. *Correlation Matrix of Selected Variables on Governance, Service Access, and Performance*

Variable	Bribery in utility	State capture	Control of corruption
Full sample			
Access to telephones [1]	0.69***	0.47***	0.66***
Access to sewerage	0.58***	0.45***	0.55***
Access to water	0.57***	0.45***	0.52***
Access to electricity	0.31**	0.27**	0.31***
Quality of infrastructure	0.79***	0.82***	0.83***
Quality of electricity	0.85***	0.77***	0.84***
Access to telephones [2]	0.83***	0.64***	0.74***
Access to cell phones	0.67***	0.57***	0.64***
Access to internet in school	0.82***	0.80***	0.88***
Average	0.68	0.58	0.66
Global city sample			
Access to telephones [1]	0.75***	0.52**	0.69***
Access to sewerage	0.57	0.38	0.52*
Access to water	0.58*	0.35	0.54*
Access to electricity	0.32	0.26*	0.37**
Quality of infrastructure	0.74***	0.76***	0.79***
Quality of electricity	0.87***	0.76***	0.84***
Access to telephones [2]	0.84***	0.60***	0.73***
Access to cell phones	0.67***	0.57***	0.59***
Access to internet in school	0.81***	0.77***	0.84***
Average	0.68	0.55	0.66
Local city sample			
Access to telephones [1]	0.58***	0.25	0.60***
Access to sewerage	0.44*	0.29	0.38***
Access to water	0.41**	0.34**	0.39***
Access to electricity	0.33*	0.32*	0.23**
Quality of infrastructure	0.67***	0.70***	0.66***
Quality of electricity	0.66***	0.51***	0.63***
Access to telephones [2]	0.71***	0.49***	0.60***
Access to cell phones	0.43***	0.22*	0.47***
Access to internet in school	0.63***	0.58***	0.81***
Average	0.54	0.41	0.53

Note: This annex complements Table 3.5. It shows pairwise correlations between selected governance variables and service access/performance variables for the full sample and for the two equal sub-samples of global and local cities. Asterisks indicate level of significance, where three is the highest level.

Annex 3.2. *Synthesis of Econometric Regression Results on Determinants of City Governance*

Dependent variables	Low bribery in utilities	Low informal money laundering	Low street crime	Red tape cost of imports	Low bribery to affect laws	Low diversion of public funds	Low illegal party financing	Low bribery in permits	Low bribery in tax	Soundness of banks	Trust in politicians	Low organized crime	Quality of postal system	Low health gap
City variables														
City population	+/'	+/'	0/0	0/0	+/0	+/'	0/0	++/'	0/0	0/0	0/0	0/0	0/0	0/0
Global city (3)	+/'	++/'***	+/'	—/'**	++/'**	++/'**	++/'***	++/'**	++/'**	+/'**	++/'***	+/'**	++/'**	+/'
Country/city size ratio	+/'	+/'	+/'	0/0	+/'	+/'	+/'	+/'	+/'	0/0	+/'	+/'	+/0	0/0
Business dummy	++/'***	+++/'***	++/'**	—/'	++/'**	+++/'***	++/'**	++/'***	++/'**	++/'**	++/'**	++/'**	++/'**	+++/'***
Website dummy	+/0	+/'	+/0	0/0	+/0	+/'	0/0	+/'	+/'	0/0	+/'	+/'	+/'	+/'
Budget dummy	0/0	+/0	+/0	0/0	—/0	0/0	0/0	0/0	0/0	+/0	—/0	0/0	+/0	0/0
Port dummy	0/0	+/'	+/0	0/0	0/0	0/0	+/'	0/0	—/'	+/0	+/0	+/0	0/0	0/0
Capital dummy	0/0	—/'	0/0	+/0	—/0	—/'	—/'	—/'	—/'	—/'	—/'	0/0	—/'	—/0
Country variables														
Country population	—/'***	—/'	—/0	++/'	—/'	—/'	—/'**	—/'***	—/'**	—/'**	—/'*	—/'	—/'	—/'***
Urbanization	++/'**	0/0	—/'	0/*	+/'	0/0	0/0	+/'	++/'	+/'	0/0	—/0	—/0	—/0
Kearney Globalization Index	++++/'***	++++/'***	++++/'***	—/'***	+++/'***	++++/'***	++++/'***	++++/'***	++++/'***	++++/'***	++++/'***	++++/'***	++++/'***	++++/'***
Income per capita	++++/'***	+++/'***	++++/'***	—/'***	++++/'***	++++/'***	+++/'***	++++/'***	++++/'***	+++/'***	++++/'***	+++/'***	++++/'***	++++/'***
Number of cities	193	193	193	193	193	193	193	193	193	193	193	193	193	193
Adjusted R^2	0.30	0.21	0.19	0.24	0.21	0.29	0.17	0.25	0.28	0.15	0.21	0.18	0.29	0.31

Note: The sample includes 412 cities in 134 countries. Values for magnitude (+, 0, -) and significance (*, 0, ') in each cell were obtained by averaging results of 21 different ordinary least squares specifications. In particular, for each independent variable, for calculating the magnitude of the coefficient rating (left-hand side), we computed the product of the average coefficient magnitude across all specifications times twice the standard deviation of the variable. Then we assigned magnitude values according to the following criteria: for positive coefficients, we applied a "++++" for any value above 1.2, "+++" for any value between 0.7 and 1.2, "++" for any value between 0.4 and 0.7, "+" for any value between 0.1 and 0.4, and finally a "0" for any value below 0.1. Similarly, minus signs were applied to negative coefficients. For the rating on the significance of the coefficient in each cell (right hand side), we averaged the various significance levels across the 21 specifications, where *** indicates significance at 1 percent, ** indicates significance at 5 percent, * indicates significance at 10 percent and ' indicates significance at 15 percent. Values for number of cities and R^2 were computed as simple averages across all specifications.

Source: All dependent variables drawn from UNCHS 1998 and World Bank 2003; globalization index downloaded from *Foreign Policy* 2002; country population and urbanization drawn from World Bank 2002, city population downloaded from website: www.citypopulation.de; port, capital, budget and business dummies drawn from Kaufmann, Léautier, and Mastruzzi 2003; control of corruption drawn from Kaufmann and Kraay 2002; Global city (3) drawn from Taylor and Walker 2001; income per capita drawn from Summers and Heston (1984) and *World Factbook* (CIA 2001); bribery in utility drawn from World Bank 2003.

Annex 3.3. *Cities in the Kaufmann-Léautier-Mastruzzi Database*

City	Located in	City	Located in
Kabul	Afghanistan	Vancouver	Canada
Tirana	Albania	Winnipeg	Canada
Algiers	Algeria	N'Djamena	Chad
Constantine	Algeria	Santiago	Chile
Oran	Algeria	Talcahuano	Chile
Reghata	Algeria	Beijing	China
Luanda	Angola	Dalian	China
Buenos Aires	Argentina	Guangzhou	China
San Fernando	Argentina	Nanjing	China
Yerevan	Armenia	Shanghai	China
Adelaida	Australia	Shenzhen	China
Brisbane	Australia	Tainjin	China
Canberra	Australia	Xiamen	China
Hobart	Australia	Barranquilla	Colombia
Melbourne	Australia	Bogota	Colombia
Perth	Australia	Manizales	Colombia
Sydney	Australia	Medellín	Colombia
Wellington	Australia	Pereira	Colombia
Linz	Austria	Kinshasa	Congo, Dem Rep.
Vienna	Austria	Alajuela	Costa Rica
Baku	Austria	Cartago	Costa Rica
Manama	Bahrain	Heredia	Costa Rica
Dhaka	Bangladesh	Cakovec	Croatia
Minsk	Belarus	Karlovac	Croatia
Antwerp	Belgium	Osijek	Croatia
Brussels	Belgium	Pula	Croatia
Waterloo	Belgium	Rijeka	Croatia
La Paz	Bolivia	Split	Croatia
Santa Cruz	Bolivia	Varazdin	Croatia
Gaborone	Botswana	Zadar	Croatia
Belo Horizonte	Brazil	Zagreb	Croatia
Brasilia	Brazil	Havana	Cuba
Curitiba	Brazil	Limassol	Cyprus
Porto Allegre	Brazil	Nicosia	Cyprus
Recife	Brazil	Prague	Czech Republic
Rio de Janeiro	Brazil	Aarhus	Denmark
Salvadore	Brazil	Copenhagen	Denmark
Saõ Paolo	Brazil	Santo Domingo	Dominican Republic
Sofia	Bulgaria	Cuenca	Ecuador
Varna	Bulgaria	Guayaquil	Ecuador
Douala	Cameroon	Ibarra	Ecuador
Yaounde	Cameroon	Quito	Ecuador
Calgary	Canada	Tenth of Ramadhan	Egypt
Edmonton	Canada	Sixth of October	Egypt
Montreal	Canada	Cairo	Egypt
Ottawa	Canada	Giza	Egypt
Québec	Canada	Antiguo Cuscatlan	El Salvador
Toronto	Canada	San Salvador	El Salvador

Annex 3.3. *(Continued)*

City	Located in	City	Located in
Tallinn	Estonia	Heyderabad	India
Tartu	Estonia	Jaipur	India
Addis Ababa	Ethiopia	Lucknow	India
Espoo	Finland	Mumbai	India
Helsinki	Finland	New Delhi	India
Lille	France	Pune	India
Lyon	France	Bandung	Indonesia
Marseilles	France	Batam	Indonesia
Paris	France	Jakarta	Indonesia
Strasbourg	France	Medan	Indonesia
Bacau	Gambia	Tehran	Iran
Banju	Gambia	Baghdad	Iraq
Kanifing	Gambia	Cork	Ireland
Serekunda	Gambia	Dublin	Ireland
Berlin	Germany	Jerusalem	Israel
Bonn	Germany	Tel Aviv	Israel
Dortmund	Germany	Belluno	Italy
Dresden	Germany	Bologna	Italy
Dusseldorf	Germany	Genoa	Italy
Essen	Germany	Milan	Italy
Frankfurt	Germany	Naples	Italy
Hamburg	Germany	Pordenone	Italy
Köln	Germany	Rome	Italy
Leipzig	Germany	Turin	Italy
Munich	Germany	Abidjan	Ivory Coast
Stuttgart	Germany	Kingston	Jamaica
Accra	Ghana	Kyoto	Japan
Tema	Ghana	Nagoya	Japan
Athens	Greece	Osaka	Japan
Guatemala City	Guatemala	Tokio	Japan
Conakry	Guinea	Yokohama	Japan
Georgetown	Guyana	Amman	Jordan
Port-au-Prince	Haiti	Almaty	Kazakhstan
La Ceiba	Honduras	Mombasa	Kenya
San Pedro Sula	Honduras	Nairobi	Kenya
Tegucigalpa	Honduras	Pyongyang	Korea, North
Villanueva	Honduras	Pusan	Korea, North
Hong Kong	Hong Kong	Seoul	Korea, North
Budapest	Hungary	Kuwait	Kuwait
Gyongyos	Hungary	Aizraukles	Latvia
Kaposvar	Hungary	Daugavpils	Latvia
Tatabanta	Hungary	Kuldiga	Latvia
Reykjavik	Iceland	Liepaja	Latvia
Ahmadabad	India	Ogre	Latvia
Bangalore	India	Riga	Latvia
Calcutta	India	Ventspils	Latvia
Chennai	India	Beirut	Lebanon
Delhi	India	Monrovia	Liberia

(table continues on following page)

Annex 3.3. *(Continued)*

City	Located in	City	Located in
Tripoli	Libya	Casablanca	Morocco
Alytus	Lithuania	Rabat	Morocco
Kaunas	Lithuania	Maputo	Mozambique
Klaipeda	Lithuania	Matola	Mozambique
Marijampole	Lithuania	Yangon	Myanmar
Panevezys	Lithuania	Windhoek	Namibia
Siualiai	Lithuania	Amsterdam	Netherlands
Silute	Lithuania	Arnhem	Netherlands
Ukmerge	Lithuania	Rotterdam	Netherlands
Vilnius	Lithuania	The Hague	Netherlands
Luxembourg	Luxembourg	Utrecht	Netherlands
Strassen	Luxembourg	Auckland	New Zealand
Macau	Macao	Christchurch	New Zealand
Bitola	Macedonia	Managua	Nicaragua
Kumahovo	Macedonia	Ikeja	Nigeria
Ohrid	Macedonia	Lagos	Nigeria
Prilep	Macedonia	Bergen	Norway
Skopje	Macedonia	Oslo	Norway
Stip	Macedonia	Stavanger	Norway
Strumica	Macedonia	Ruwi	Oman
Veles	Macedonia	Islamabad	Pakistan
Antananarivo	Madagascar	Karachi	Pakistan
Toamasina	Madagascar	Lahore	Pakistan
Blantyre	Malawi	Rawalpindi	Pakistan
Lilongwe	Malawi	Panama City	Panama
Kuala Lumpur	Malaysia	Asuncion	Paraguay
Labuan	Malaysia	Ciudad del Este	Paraguay
Malaca	Malaysia	FDO de la Mora	Paraguay
Penang	Malaysia	Santa Rita	Paraguay
Petaling Jaya	Malaysia	Callao	Peru
Shah Alam	Malaysia	Lima	Peru
Bamako	Mali	Ho-Pasig	Philippines
Ségou	Mali	Makati	Philippines
Floriana	Malta	Manila	Philippines
Gzira	Malta	Paranaque	Philippines
Marsa	Malta	Warsaw	Poland
San Gwann	Malta	Lisbon	Portugal
Sliema	Malta	Doha	Qatar
Valletta	Malta	Alba Iulia	Romania
Zejtun	Malta	Bucarest	Romania
Port Louis	Mauritius	Constanta	Romania
Guadalajara	Mexico	Cariova	Romania
Mexico City	Mexico	Iasi	Romania
Monterrey	Mexico	Oradea	Romania
San Pedro Garza G.	Mexico	Piatra Neamt	Romania
Tijuana	Mexico	Ploiesti	Romania
Torreon	Mexico	Ramnico Valcea	Romania
Xalapa	Mexico	Slatina	Romania

Annex 3.3. *(Continued)*

City	Located in	City	Located in
Targoviste	Romania	Babebo	Serbia and Montenegro
Camapa	Russia	Belgrade	Serbia and Montenegro
Moscow	Russia	Kraljevo	Serbia and Montenegro
St. Petersburg	Russia	Nis	Serbia and Montenegro
Jeddah	Saudi Arabia	Novi Sad	Serbia and Montenegro
Riyadh	Saudi Arabia	Sr. Mitrovica	Serbia and Montenegro
Dakar	Senegal	Subotica	Serbia and Montenegro
Freetown	Sierra Leone	Uzice	Serbia and Montenegro
Singapore	Singapore	Couva	Trinidad & Tobago
Bratislava	Slovak Rep.	Port of Spain	Trinidad & Tobago
Presov	Slovak Rep.	Sfax	Tunisia
Previdza	Slovak Rep.	Sousse	Tunisia
Celje	Slovenia	Tunis	Tunisia
Kranj	Slovenia	Ankara	Turkey
Ljubljana	Slovenia	Balikesir	Turkey
Marobor	Slovenia	Instanbul	Turkey
Murska Sobota	Slovenia	Kampala	Uganda
Novo Mesto	Slovenia	Kueb	Ukraine
Slovenj Gradec	Slovenia	Abu Dhabi	United Arab Emirates
Cape Town	South Africa	Dubai	United Arab Emirates
Durban	South Africa	Birmingham	United Kingdom
Johannesburg	South Africa	Bristol	United Kingdom
Midrand	South Africa	Cardiff	United Kingdom
Pretoria	South Africa	Edingburgh	United Kingdom
Barcelona	Spain	Glasgow	United Kingdom
Bilbao	Spain	Leeds	United Kingdom
Madrid	Spain	Liverpool	United Kingdom
Seville	Spain	London	United Kingdom
Valencia	Spain	Manchester	United Kingdom
Colombo	Sri Lanka	Newcastle	United Kingdom
Mount Lavinia	Sri Lanka	Nottingham	United Kingdom
Khartoum	Sudan	Alexandria	United States
Gothenburg	Sweden	Atlanta	United States
Stockholm	Sweden	Baltimore	United States
Basel	Switzerland	Boston	United States
Geneva	Switzerland	Buffalo	United States
St. Gallen	Switzerland	Charlotte	United States
Zurich	Switzerland	Chicago	United States
Damascus	Syria	Cincinnati	United States
Kaohsiung	Taiwan	Cleveland	United States
Taichung	Taiwan	Columbus	United States
Taipei	Taiwan	Dallas	United States
Arusha	Tanzania	Denver	United States
Dar es Salaam	Tanzania	Detroit	United States
Morogoro	Tanzania	Houston	United States
Bangkok	Thailand	Kansas City	United States
Lome	Togo	Los Angeles	United States
Arima	Trinidad & Tobago	Miami	United States

(table continues on following page)

Annex 3.3. *(Continued)*

City	Located in	City	Located in
Minneapolis	United States	Wilmington	United States
New Orleans	United States	Montevideo	Uruguay
New York	United States	Tashkent	Uzbekistan
Philadelphia	United States	Caracas	Venezuela
Phoenix	United States	Beinhoa	Vietnam
Pittsburg	United States	Hanoi	Vietnam
Portland	United States	Ho Chi Minh	Vietnam
Richmond	United States	Sana'a	Yemen
San Diego	United States	Kitwe	Zambia
San Francisco	United States	Lusaka	Zambia
San Jose	United States	Ndola	Zambia
Seattle	United States	Bulawayo	Zimbabwe
St Louis	United States	Harare	Zimbabwe
Washington	United States		

Notes

The margins of error in any governance, institutional quality and urban dataset imply that interpretative caution is warranted in general, and in particular argue against inferring seemingly precise city or country rankings from the data. For details on data, visit: http://www.worldbank.org/wbi/governance/.

1. Because of the dynamic nature of data entry into the internet, these search percentages are valid at the time of the search, which was April 2004.

2. See Annex 3.4 for the list of cities in the current version of the database. We use various sources of data for this analysis, detailed in the annex. First, a comprehensive city level data set is taken from the UN Urban Observatory, which has data on 232 cities in 114 countries for 1998. We refer to this database as the UN database. We also use data from the GaWC research, which we call the Taylor database, which includes a roster of 265 cities constructed from data on the number of firms (advertising, accounting, banking, and law) and number of practitioners/offices in 265 cities for 2000. We construct a special database, which we refer to as the KLM (Kaufmann, Léautier, Mastruzzi) database and which includes data in 412 cities from 134 countries for 2003, based in large part on a worldwide enterprise survey (EOS). This database consists of 36 variables of governance, as well as city and country economic data.

3. The expanded city level dataset includes over a hundred variables. However, since part of this consolidated dataset is aggregated from different existing data sources comprising a different set of cities, the consolidated dataset contains many missing values. One of the objectives for the future is to build up this city level dataset and fill in these data gaps.

4. Kyu Sik Lee and Alex Anas in "The Benefits of Alternative Power Tariffs for Nigeria and Indonesia" (1996), demonstrate how companies locate in a city and if they do not find the services they need either invest in their own generation, thereby exiting the system, or put pressure to get better services, with potential improvements in local governance, or relocate to cities with better services.

5. The Taylor database gives us data on financial and banking companies located in a city, as well as data on the availability of key companies in law, accounting, and advertising, all measures of indicators (a), (d), and (f) in the Friedman (1986) hypothesis. From the UN and KLM databases we get measures of key infrastructure endowments (indicator (b)). City size (indicator (c)) is obtained from the website: http://www.citypopulation.de. We use the Kearney composite measure of globalization for measure (e) and have collected web statistics that show whether a city has a website and if it posts budget information or business information there to capture the Townsend (2001) indicators. The only measure we do not use in our analysis is the presence of international institutions in the city.

6. In the sense of "Popperian falsifiability," taking the second definition of global city as is would not be very useful to test the hypothesis that global cities perform better. Thus, we obviate such a problem by interpreting the first definition as a potential input and the second definition as an outcome (to be empirically tested).

7. The UNCHS Expert Group Meeting on Urban Poverty and Governance Indicators, April 29 to May 1, 1999, in Nairobi, Kenya, highlights the top 12 indicators of urban governance: (a) consumer satisfaction; (b) openness of procedures for contracts/tenders for municipal services; (c) equity in the tax system; (d) sources of

local government funding (taxes, user charges, borrowing, central government, international aid); (e) percentage of population served by services; (f) access of public to stages of policy cycle; (g) fairness in enforcing laws; (h) incorporation of excluded groups in the consultation process; (i) clarity of procedures and regulations and responsibilities; (j) existing participatory processes; (k) freedom of the media and existence of local media; and (l) autonomy of financial resources.

8. This would permit, inter alia, to answer questions such as: Do cities and countries that have an improving trend in governance also continue to perform better in terms of their degree of globalization and their ability to translate global opportunities into local value or both?, Would the scale of a city be a good measure of such a phenomenon?

9. Taylor defines alpha cities as those with global significance in four key global city functions (international accountancy, advertising, banking, and legal services). A beta city is one that has global significance in three of the four key world-city (global city) functions. A gamma city is one that has global significance in two of the four key global city functions. Using the network aspects of the GaWC is a key advantage that we consider in looking at the issue of governance, asking questions like: Are less globalized cities relatively less well governed than global cities and therefore trail even further behind? We group cities into two categories of "global" and "local" to present some of the results in charts that visually capture the main empirical findings.

10. Specifically, in this index economic integration combines data on trade, foreign direct investment (FDI), and portfolio capital flows, as well as investment income payments and receipts. Personal contact tracks international travel and tourism, international telephone traffic, and cross-border remittances and personal transfers (including worker remittances, compensation to employees, and other person-to-person and nongovernmental transfers). Technological connectivity counts the number of internet users, internet hosts, and secure servers through which encrypted transactions are carried out. Finally, political engagement tracks each country's memberships in international organizations, personnel and financial contributions to U.N. Security Council missions, ratification of selected multilateral international treaties, and the amount of governmental transfer payments and receipts.

11. Access of the population to telephones is also referred to here as "access to telephones 1"; access of businesses to telephones is also referred to as "access to telephones 2."

12. Telephone access in Tables 3.2 and 3.3 seems to show overall a higher difference than other services. This may be because telecommunications, which is also a voice-enhancing tool, is rather important for transparency. A more globalized city with better telecommunications services may offer better opportunities for voice, both local and international, and hence derive more transparency. Such a result has been envisaged by some researchers (see Sassen 2002).

13. In particular, for each independent variable, for calculating the magnitude of the coefficient rating (left-hand side), we computed the product of the average coefficient magnitude across all specifications times twice the standard deviation of the variable. Then we assigned magnitude values according to the following criteria: for positive coefficients, we applied a "++++" for any value above 1.2; "+++" for any value between 0.7 and 1.2; "++" for any value between 0.4 and 0.7; "+" for any

value between 0.1 and 0.4; and finally a "0" for any value below 0.1. Similarly, minus signs were applied to negative coefficients. For the rating on the significance of the coefficient in each cell (right hand side), we averaged the various significance levels across the 21 specifications, where *** indicates significance at 1 percent, ** indicates significance at 5 percent, * indicates significance at 10 percent and ' indicates significance at 15 percent.

14. We have presented synthesis results and have not shown the results of multiple correlations. We also have chosen to use data plots and not the actual econometric results. The actual regressions were tested for sign switches, and except for the access to electricity variable, the regressions did not show sign switches for the key variables. This is why we thought it best to show the range of coefficient estimates and the statistical significance. All the synthesis tables we have developed present controlled statistical results, as opposed to bivariate regressions, even if shown only in synthesis form.

15. In essence we could conceptualize of another hypothesis, where the ability of cities to translate global opportunity into local value depends on governance, and that cities compete with each other on the basis of governance and not on the basis of initial endowments (infrastructure, culture, etc.). Cities with better governance remain globalized for longer periods of time (attract higher flows of capital, people, firms, finance, products) or attract such flows systemically over time (growth or change in volumes of these flows over time). This test would allow us to distinguish between those cities that are highly global and then drop in their rankings over time. For such a test, we would need at least two time periods. A possible model specification could include:

$$\Delta Y = f(X_1, X_2, X_3) + \varepsilon$$

where ΔY = change in the vector of governance indicators, to capture improvements or deterioration in governance over time which is a proxy for staying power in translating global opportunity to local value; X_1 = a dummy for an alpha city from the Taylor database; X_2 = dummy for a beta city, and X_3 = dummy for a gamma city. With such a specification one could investigate whether alpha and beta type cities have better governance compared to the gamma type cities.

16. Other areas of investigation could include looking at the influence of diaspora networks on the governance of a city, as well as the influence of NGO movements for instance on human rights, environment, and corporate social responsibility issues within the context of the city, and its links to public governance. Further, expanding on the research on the interface between technology choices, governance and city performance also appear to be a promising line of inquiry from an empirical standpoint, which is addressed in Chapter 6.

17. This would imply that the World Bank and other international financial institutions work with intercity governance alliances and networks, such as the association of local governments and Cities Alliance, a city-to-city partnership.

References

Acemoglu, D., S. Johnson, and J. Robinson. 2003. "Understanding Prosperity and Poverty: Geography, Institutions and the Reversal of Fortune." NBER Working Paper 8460. Cambridge, MA: National Bureau of Economic Research.

Castells, M. 2000. "Materials for an exploratory theory of the network society." *British Journal of Sociology* 51: 5–24.

CIA (Central Intelligence Agency). 2001. *World Factbook 2001.* On-line at http://www.cia.gov/cia/publications/factbook/.

Deas, I., and B. Giordano. 2001. "Conceptualizing and Measuring Urban Competitiveness in Major English Cities." *Environment and Planning* A 33: 1411–1429.

De Long, J. Bradford, and A. Shleifer. 1992. "Princes and Merchants: European City Growth Before the Industrial Revolution." December 1992. Cambridge, MA: National Bureau of Economic Research and Harvard University.

Doel, M. A., and P. J. Hubbard. 2002. "Taking World Cities Literally: Marketing the City in a Global Space of Flows." *City* 6(3).

Foreign Policy. 2002. A. T. Kearney/Foreign Policy Magazine Globalization Index 2002. On-line at http://www.foreignpolicy.com/wwwboard/g-index2.php. Released as "Globalization's Last Hurrah." *Foreign Policy* (Jan/Feb): 38–51.

Friedmann, J. 1986. "The World City Hypothesis." Development and Change 17: 69–83.

Kaufmann, D., and A. Kraay. 2002. "Growth without Governance." *Economia* 3(1): 169–229. On-line at http://www.worldbank.org/wbi/governance/pubs/growthgov.html.

Kaufmann, D., A. Kraay, and M. Mastruzzi. 2003. *Governance Matters III: Governance Indicators for 1996–2002.* World Bank Policy Research Working Paper 3106. Washington, DC: World Bank.

Kaufmann, D., F. Léautier, and M. Mastruzzi. 2003. Database on Urban Indicators. Washington, DC: World Bank. Available from authors upon request.

Kaufmann, D., M. Mastruzzi, and D. Zavaleta. 2003. "Sustained Macroeconomic Reform, Tepid Growth: A Governance Puzzle in Bolivia." Chapter 12 in D. Rodrik, ed., *In Search of Prosperity: Analytic Narratives on Economic Growth.* Princeton NJ: Princeton University Press.

Knack, S., and P. Keefer. 1997. "Does Social Capital Have an Economic Payoff? A Cross Country Investigation." *Quarterly Journal of Economics* 112(4): 1251–1288.

Knox, P. L. 2002. "World Cities and the Organization of Global Space." Pages 328-338 in P. J. Taylor and M. J. Watts, eds., *Geographies of Global Change,* 2d ed. Oxford: Blackwell.

Kresl, P. 1995. "The Determinants of Urban Competitiveness: a Survey." In Kresl, P., and G. Gappert, eds., *North American Cities and the Global Economy.* Beverly Hills, CA: Sage.

Lee, K. S., and A. Anas. 1996. "The Benefits of Alternative Power Tariffs for Nigeria and Indonesia." World Bank Policy Research Working Paper 1606. Washington, DC: World Bank.

Mehta, D. 1998. "Urban Governance: Lessons from Best Practices in Asia." UMP-Asia Occasional Paper No. 40. United Nations Urban Management Program Regional Office for Asia and the Pacific, Bangkok.

Progressive Living. 2005. Definition of globalization. On-line at http://www.proressive living.org.

Sassen, S. 2000. "Locating Cities on Global Circuits." GaWC Research Bulletin No. 46. On-line at http://www.lboro.ac.uk/gawc/rb/rb46.html.

———. 2002. "Global Cities and Diasporic Networks: Microsites in Global Civil Society." Chapter 9 in *Global Civil Society 2002*. London: Centre for the Study of Global Governance.

Short, J., and others. 1996. "The dirty little secret of World City research-data problems in comparative analysis." *International Journal of Urban and Regional Research* 20: 697-719.

Smith, D. A., and M. Timberlake. 1995. "Conceptualizing and Mapping the Structure of the World Systems City System." *Urban Studies* 32: 287-302.

Summers, R., and A. Heston. 1984. "Improved International Comparisons of Real Product and its Composition, 1950-80." Review of Income and Wealth 207-61. World Bank. Various years. *World Development Indicators*. Washington, DC.

Taylor, P. J, and D. R. F. Walker. 2001. "World City Network: Data Matrix Construction and Analysis." Online at http://www.lboro.ac.uk/gawc/. From the GaWC Research Group and Network, Data Set 6, and based on primary data collected by J. V. Beaverstock, R. G. Smith, and P. J. Taylor (Economic and Social Research Council project "The Geographical Scope of London as a World City").

Tiebout, Charles M. 1956. "A Pure Theory of Local Expenditures." *Journal of Political Economy* 64: 416–424.

Townsend, A. 2001. "The Internet and the Rise of the New Network Cities." *Environment and Planning B: Planning and Design* 28: 39-58.

UNCHS (United Nations Commission on Human Settlements). 1998. Global Urban Indicators Database. On-line at http:/www/unhabitat.org/programmes/guo/guo_indicators.asp.

———. 1999. "UNCHS Expert Meeting on Urban Poverty and Governance Indicators." 29 April to May 1999, Nairobi Kenya. On-line at http://www.gdrc.org/u-gov/indicators.html. Determinants of City Governance—Synthesis of Econometric Regression Results.

UNESCO. 2000. Definition of urban governance. On-line at http://www.unesco.org/most/most2.htm.

World Bank. 2002. *World Development Indicators 2002*. Washington, DC.

———. 2003. Enterprise Outreach Services (EOS) Database. Washington, DC.

World Economic Forum. Various years. "Executive Opinion Survey." Geneva. Prepared for *The Global Competitiveness Report*.

4

Urban Performance Profiles: The Impact of Globalization and the Challenge for Africa

Frannie Léautier and Barjor Mehta

Globalization is a phenomenon that has been going on for centuries, but its speed has picked up in the past 40 years. Cities find themselves in a global space where they are asked to compete with each other—even without desiring to do so. Globalization seems to favor cities that are already relatively strong, at the expense of those that are weak. Some hypotheses suggest that strong cities grow stronger, while weak cities seem to get weaker—unless they undertake corrective actions. These must be actions designed to propel the weaker cities into the ranks of cities considered to have good business addresses or to be great places to visit or reside. City managers and urban policy makers respond to these hypotheses, which are many times founded on weak empirical evidence. They seem to assume that global businesses favor cities with strong performance in matters such as infrastructure services, quality of life indicators, and human resources.

In this chapter we use an empirical approach to examine whether the influx of global business, including connections with international markets, tends on balance to improve or degrade existing city performance. City managers and national policy makers intent on seeking economic growth by joining the global economy will benefit from knowing what specific interventions—enhancing services and human resources, for example—are most likely to attract the kind of global activities, such as finance, trade, and tourism, that will complement rather than tax their cities' existing strengths.

To do this, we use two sets of empirical explorations. First, we compare city performance profiles on a number of dimensions, asking whether globalization does indeed seem to favor well-performing cities. Second, we look at the specific case of Africa, to see if urban dynamics in Africa are the same or different in comparison with cities elsewhere.

Globalization and City Performance

When companies or citizens choose a city in which to locate, they pay attention to issues such as the quality of life and access to critical infrastructural and social services. Observed city performance profiles, therefore, exhibit mutual interdependence between the attained level of globalization and the performance of the city—unless city managers are not responsive to signals from firms or citizens. Such a case would occur if cities are badly governed, or if the levers that city managers can use are few.

Several authors have looked at the issue of urban governance in the context of globalization (Kaufmann, Léautier, and Mastruzzi 2004) and in the context of an evolving interaction between city managers on the one hand, and firms and citizens on the other (Dingham and Léautier 2005; Lo and Yeung 1998). Others have looked at the scope of local governments and their capacity to intervene in policy and service decisions at the city level (Campbell 2003). In this chapter, we first seek empirical evidence that suggests there is a possibility for local city managers to intervene to improve their cities' performances. We examine whether this capacity to respond varies across cities with different degrees of globalization.

There are many definitions of globalization including economic, social, political, cultural, and physical globalization. Economic globalization is determined by the activities of multinationals, as well as by transport and logistics links, the flow of exports, and tourism trends. Social globalization is determined on the basis of such issues as gaps between the number and perspectives of youth and the elderly, skills and education gaps across generations and communities, labor standards and employment conditions, economic migrants, health issues such as HIV/AIDS, malaria, and tuberculosis, and differential access to income, information, and technology. Political globalization considers political links among cities due to company location, trade links, media access and interest, investment flows, and the changing relationship between the state and the individual, as well as the state and the global markets. Cultural globalization examines the importance of international television, film, music, sports, shopping opportunities, casinos, restaurants, bars, and so on. Physical globalization (sometimes called regionalization) considers sprawl beyond city and country boundaries, distributed and linked services, the decline of hubs or cores and the simultaneous growth of small cities and megacities. There is a rich body of research addressing how globalization has impacted urban corridors, new technologies, transport and telecommunications, financial centers, and Islamic cities (Lo and Yeung 1998). Research has also explored the specific problems of African cities in an era of globalization (Rakodi 1997).

For purposes of this chapter we use an index of globalization developed by A. T. Kearney and *Foreign Policy* (*Foreign Policy* 2003). This index is calculated by assessing changes in the components of globalization measured by:

- *Political engagement:* the number of memberships in international organizations, UN Security Council missions in which each country participates, and foreign embassies that each country hosts.
- *Technology:* the number of internet users, internet hosts, and secure servers.
- *Personal contact:* international travel and tourism, international telephone traffic, and cross-border transfers.
- *Economic integration:* trade, foreign direct investment and portfolio capital flows, and income payments and receipts.

The A.T. Kearney Globalization Index for 2003 tracked these changes across 62 advanced economies and emerging markets to draw a picture of globalization across all the world's regions. The Globalization Index list of countries was then matched with the countries for which the United Nations Human Settlements Programme (HABITAT) has collected city-level data (UNCHS 1998). For this study, we eliminated the advanced economies and those countries for which there was nothing in the city database. This resulted in a final list of 30 countries and 86 cities ranked in order of the Kearney Index and grouped in two sets, with a corresponding list of 46 cities in highly globalized countries and 40 cities in less-globalized countries. The distribution of countries and cities in the data set we use are attached in Annex 4.1.

We use the city-level data from the UNCHS database to examine the relationship between globalization as determined by the A. T. Kearney Index and city performance. In measuring performance, we look at seven key factors: (a) economic performance as measured by city product per capita, average per capita income, and the share of informal employment; (b) city characteristics as measured by residential density, population growth rates, and average household size; (c) equity in cities as measured by the share of households below the poverty line and by income disparity; (d) how a city performs with respect to infrastructure services as measured by city transportation services and waste management; (e) the capacity to provide social services, such as the mortality rates for children less than five years old, the number of hospital beds per capita, and the number of children per primary and secondary classroom; (f) the performance of city local governments as measured by local government revenue and expenditures per capita, and wages in the local government budget; and (g) urban crime as measured by theft and murder rates at the city level, which are indicators of security.

We hypothesize that city managers will have less direct control over the first three of these factors than they will have over the last four factors. Hence, cities with active city management should have significantly higher performance in the last four indicators, in comparison with the first three, if they are highly globalized and if everything else is equal.

The starting hypotheses are that cities of more-globalized countries should be more efficient and provide better quality of life as they respond to competitive global business pressures. Firms and individuals choosing to locate in a city should be sensitive to indicators such as higher densities, quality of transport services, access to water and electricity, as well as to security, and hence we expect to see that these indicator levels are higher in more-globalized cities. However, it is not clear how cities of more-globalized countries will fare as they respond to the pressures of their local citizens for health and education services, for example, which are more local in nature. These services depend on the quality of local institutions. We would expect to see a large variance across city performance profiles in cities at the same level of globalization, if this hypothesis holds.

City Profiles: Where Cities Have Little Control

We compare the city profiles of more-globalized and less-globalized cities on the three categories of performance over which we hypothesize city managers have relatively little control. The data are attached in Annex 4.1.

Economic Performance of Cities

In Table 4.1, we use three indicators of growth and productivity to examine how urban local governments rate on measures of economic performance: (a) city product in U.S. dollars per capita per year; (b) the average per capita income, as a measure of wealth creation; and (c) the ability to create jobs in the formal sector as measured by the share of employment that is informal.

From the data, we see that there is empirical evidence that more-globalized countries have cities that perform better economically, producing more and offering their citizens opportunities for higher average incomes. City product per capita is three times higher in more-globalized cities than in less-globalized cities. Average per capita income is five times higher in more-globalized cities. Such cities also seem to provide more formal employment opportunities than their less-globalized counterparts.[1]

City Characteristics

When one travels to a city or looks for data about it, one is always curious to know about city density and other characteristics that are determinants of the quality of life. Table 4.2 shows that cities in countries that are more globalized have lower residential densities as measured in persons per hectare. Cities located in more-globalized countries also seem to be growing more slowly and have lower average household sizes. This may indicate that living conditions in such cities are less stressed than their counterparts in less-globalized countries. Could such results indicate that the quality of life in such cities is higher because they are less dense, offer more space per person, are not growing as fast, and may be less congested? Are these cities also those that have achieved higher levels of services, with well functioning local governments?

Equity

Does globalization affect equity? Traveling around the world, people are affected by the visual difference in income disparity in cities, whether it is at the neighborhood level or across the whole city. We look at two indicators of equity: (a) households below the poverty line, which is a measure of how well cities are providing for their poorer residents; and (b) income disparity as measured by the ratio of the fifth lowest income quintile to the highest quintile (Table 4.3).

Cities in more-globalized countries have about the same share of households living below the poverty line, compared with the cities in less-globalized countries. However, income disparities are much lower in cities in more-globalized countries. This result may indicate that cities in more-globalized countries receive better instruments for dealing with inequities then cities in less-globalized countries, as

Table 4.1. *Economic Performance of Cities, 1993*

	Cities in countries that are	
Indicator	More globalized	Less globalized
City product per capita (1993 US$)	3,818	1,175
Average per capita income (Quintile 3 per person in US$)	2,066	377
Informal employment (percent)	32	40

Source: UNCHS 1998, Global Urban Indicators.

Table 4.2. *Residential Density, Growth Rates, and Household Size, 1993*

	Cities in countries that are	
Indicator	More globalized	Less globalized
Residential density (persons/ha)	96	252
Annual population growth rates (percent)	2	3
Average household size (persons)	3	5

Source: UNCHS 1998, Global Urban Indicators.

Table 4.3. Equity in Cities, 1993

	Cities in countries that are	
Indicator	More globalized	Less globalized
Households below poverty line (percent)	26	27
Income disparity (Quintile 5/Quintile 1)	7	12

Source: UNCHS 1998, Global Urban Indicators.

Table 4.4. City Transportation, 1993

	Cities in countries that are	
Indicator	More globalized	Less globalized
Mean travel time to work (minutes)	30	35
Modes of travel to work (% of total work trips)		
Private car	25	10
Train/tram	14	7
Bus/mini bus	23	37
Motorcycle	4	12
Bicycle	11	7
On foot	24	22
Other	2	13

Note: Percentages do not add to 100 due to rounding.
Source: UNCHS 1998, Global Urban Indicators.

they tend to be richer. Cities in less-globalized countries may not be at a level where the benefits of globalization can be used to reduce the number of poor people or to reduce income disparities.

City Profiles: Where Cities Have More Control

Cities do tend to have more control over the provision of local urban public services, such as transport, waste collection, social services, and security at the city level. Do cities in more-globalized countries have a better quality of services?

Quality of City Transportation and Waste Management Services

In Table 4.4, we see that cities of more-globalized countries offer shorter commutes to work. This could be related to lower urban densities because the more dense the city, the greater the number of commuters, and hence the longer the commute. However, the work commute also depends on the size and structure of the city, since urban sprawl affects the time involved, and on the types of transportation services available. Table 4.4 shows commute patterns by mode of transportation. We see that cities of more-globalized countries offer more choices to their residents, including private cars, trains or trams, bicycles, or a commute on foot.

Compare this pattern to less-globalized cities that are highly dependent on bus transport and motorcycles. It is possible that the low mean travel time to work in cities of more-globalized countries results from a combination of lower densities and the availability of choices that residents can utilize. If so, this is an indicator of a more varied and efficient service.

Table 4.5. City Waste Management Services, 1993

	Cities in countries that are	
Indicator	More globalized	Less globalized
Solid waste generated per capita (tons per year)	0.5	0.4
Regular waste collection (from % of households)	77	68
Waste water treated (% of generated)	52	68
Solid waste disposal methods (% of total disposed)		
Landfills	28	35
Incinerator	11	7
Open dump	42	45
Recycling	8	10
Other	12	9

Source: UNCHS 1998, Global Urban Indicators.

These results provide support for the idea that the presence of globalized enti-ties, such as foreign firms and internationally mobile individuals, may put pressure on cities to deliver better services in the area of transportation, or that firms may locate in cities with better infrastructure services. Do the results hold for other types of services that are visible to the visitor's eyes or services that are proven to be important when people decide to locate in a particular city?

We ask these questions of the data because it is not easy to observe the quality of institutions. One can observe, however, the results of service provision decisions made by local institutions and use them to make judgments. A visitor to a city for purposes of investment or for tourism might be interested in the quality of services, such as transport and solid waste collection, and also in security measures includ-ing both petty theft and major crime. We check to see if these types of services are also better provided by cities in countries that are more globalized. The results are presented in Table 4.5.

While cities of more-globalized countries produce more waste than those in less-globalized countries, they do a better job of collecting waste. However, cities in less-globalized countries show a higher average in treating waste. The methods of treat-ing city waste in more-globalized countries are not significantly more advanced than in less-globalized ones. Unlike transportation services, which are more visible when they do not work, waste disposal is less evident. Citizens care more about the fact that waste is collected in their neighborhoods than how it is treated after it is trans-ported out of sight. While cities of more-globalized countries do use more incinera-tion than less-globalized ones and rely less on open dumps than the less-globalized cities, they use recycling less frequently. The reuse of plastic, glass, paper, and metal in cities of the less-globalized countries is very high and is obvious in the large num-ber of people who are employed in this sector in such countries.

Quality of City Social Services

What about social services? Are they better provided in cities of more-globalized countries? In Table 4.6 we see that in more-globalized countries cities indeed have better outcomes in the provision of all health and education services. This may be an indication that such cities do have sufficient local political pressure to deal with local problems, such as health and education.

Performance of Local Governments

Using a number of indicators for local government performance, the data show that capital expenditure and revenues collected per capita by local urban governments are higher for cities in more-globalized countries (Table 4.7). This result supports the hypothesis that with globalization there is more spending by local governments on their cities, as they try to provide a higher level of civic services.

In addition, local government wages in cities of more-globalized countries make up a smaller share of the local budget. This result could indicate that local urban governments perform more efficiently in countries that are more globalized. In a paper by Kaufmann, Léautier, and Mastruzzi (2004) this hypothesis is formally tested and supported, using a rich data set (see also Chapter 3).

Crime and Security

Indicators of security impact a city's local economy and the perception of its quality of life. Table 4.8 shows that cities in countries that are more globalized tend to have lower levels of murder but have a greater incidence of theft than cities in less-globalized countries. This indicator of security may be differentiated by neighborhood but, with the data we have, we are unable to test whether such differentiation holds.

Table 4.6. *Health and Education in Cities, 1993*

Indicator	Cities in countries that are	
	More globalized	*Less globalized*
Child mortality (% of children < 5 yrs)	4	6
Persons per hospital bed	144	528
Children per primary classroom	38	43
Children per secondary classroom	36	44

Source: UNCHS 1998, Global Urban Indicators.

Table 4.7. *Urban Local Government Revenue and Capital Expenditure, 1993*

Indicator	Cities in countries that are	
	More globalized	*Less globalized*
Local government revenue per capita (1993 US$ per year)	266	115
Local government capital expenditure per capita (1993 US$ per year)	104	22
Wages in the local government budget (%)	21	38

Source: UNCHS 1998, Global Urban Indicators.

Table 4.8. Urban Crime, 1993

Indicator	Cities in countries that are	
	More globalized	Less globalized
Murders (per thousand population)	0.1	0.6
Thefts (per thousand population)	14	5

Source: UNCHS 1998, Global Urban Indicators.

Table 4.9. Differences in Performance Profiles of More-globalized and Less-globalized Cities

City performance profile	Average difference between more- and less-globalized cities (percent)	Variance between more- and less-globalized cities
Economic performance	42	0.34
City characteristics	−78	0.57
Equity	−38	0.25
Transportation services	−100	5.63
Waste management services	−1	0.07
Health and education services	−86	1.46
Local government finances	19	0.74
Urban crime	−313	29.93

Source: Data in Annex 4.2.

City versus National Levels of Control

To test the hypothesis that cities have more control over outcomes involving local government, revenue and expenditure, and urban crime than they do over economic performance, city characteristics, or equity, we compare the average difference and variance in city performance for all the indicators discussed here. The results are shown in Table 4.9 (for details see Annex 4.2).

It is interesting to note that the hypothesis is supported for the most part. City managers seem to have more leverage over the performance of their cities when it comes to issues such as transportation services, including congestion as measured by travel time to work and options for public transportation. The same is also generally true in the areas of health and education services, as well as urban crime. Both the average difference and variance in these indicators of city performance are higher when comparing cities in more-globalized countries to those in less-globalized countries.

For the other indicators, cities seem to have less control, as the average differences in performance and variance are lower. One exception is city characteristics, such as city density, with a high average difference, albeit with low observed variance. We suspect that city managers are able to manage city density through zoning, even if they cannot control city density through provision of large-scale infrastructure, for which they may depend on national governments.

City Performance Profiles across Regions

Since we find support for the hypothesis that cities in more-globalized countries tend to have better performance profiles than those in less-globalized countries, we want to see if these results hold even after controlling for regional differences.

Figure 4.1. *Urban and Rural Populations of the Developed and Developing Worlds, 1950–2030 (billions of people)*

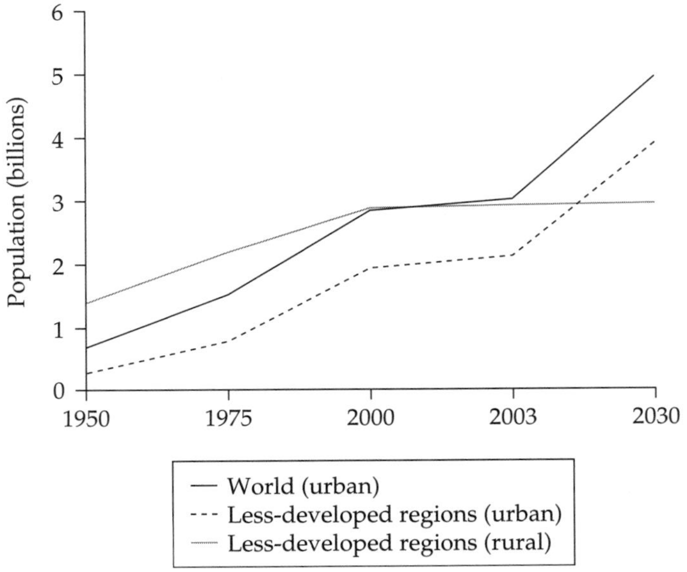

Source: UNDESA 2004.

Urbanization rates have been high globally, but the highest growth has been in developing countries. Cities of all sizes, whether mega, large, or small, have been growing. Despite this high growth, many urban residents still do not have access to basic services, and a large number of poor live in urban centers around the world.

According to the United Nations, in 2003 48 percent of the world's population lived in urban areas, a figure that is projected to exceed the 50 percent mark by 2007 (UNDESA 2004). The global urban population was estimated at 3 billion in 2003 and is expected to rise to 5 billion by 2030 (Figure 4.1).

What about Africa?

For many years the focus of urban studies has been on Asia and its large and fast-growing cities. Only recently, researchers have begun to examine the multiple critical stresses faced by rapid urban growth but weak globalization across Africa (Simon 1997). While there is debate on the accuracy of the data on Africa because of an inconsistency of census rounds across several countries of the continent, no one doubts the grave situation that is unfolding in cities and towns across the African continent. The authors believe that considering the fairly accurate population projections presented by the United Nations in the past, current data on urbanization prospects from the same source have to be taken very seriously.

At around 3.3 to 3.7 percent annually, African urban population growth rates have been and will continue to be the highest in the world. African city-based populations are growing faster than their counterparts in Asia. These higher growth rates, compared with other regions of the world, are expected to continue well into the next two decades (Table 4.10). As a result of the very rapid rate of growth, the absolute number of people living in Africa's cities is expected to exceed the rural

Table 4.10. *Average Annual Growth of the Urban Population, by Region, 1995–2000 and Projected for 2000–2015*
(percent)

Region	1995–2000	2000–2005	2005–2010	2010–2015
Africa	3.8	3.6	3.4	3.2
Asia	2.90	2.67	2.50	2.3
Europe	0.2	0.1	0.1	0.1
Latin America and the Caribbean	2.2	2.0	1.7	1.5
North America	1.5	1.4	1.3	1.2

Source: UNDESA 2004.

Table 4.11. *Extent of Urbanization, by Region, 2000, 2003, and Projected for 2030*
(percent)

Region	2000	2003	2030
Africa	37	39	54
Asia	37	38	53
Europe	73	73	80
Latin America and the Caribbean	76	77	85
North America	73	73	75

Source: UNDESA 2004.

population by the year 2030 (Table 4.11). These projections hold despite a general slowdown in urbanization across the world; urban growth in 2000–2005 is lower than that experienced in 1995–2000.

Severe problems associated with rapid urban growth across Africa have to be seen in the context of existing local urban conditions there. Across all city-level urban indicators—city crime rates, travel to work times, waste collection and treatment, health and education situations, urban local government revenues, and local economic performance—African cities appear to perform well below their counterparts in the developing world (Table 4.12).

Many African countries are characterized today by population concentrations in one or two major cities; however, there is a rapid growth of medium and small cities in almost all countries in Africa. The unprecedented accelerated pace and extent of urban growth in African cities, with a huge backlog of demand for services and hard infrastructure, will continue to exert increasingly extreme pressure on African national and local policies, as well as approaches to urbanization. At a similar time in Asia's developmental timeline, rapid urbanization was accompanied by supportive economic growth, and therefore, to some extent, many Asian countries were able to put supportive structures in place. Unfortunately, this is not true for Africa. Urban growth in Africa does not seem to be accompanied by corresponding economic growth. This creates a very special dilemma (Fay and Opal 2000). While the design and implementation of effective plans and initiatives at the level of local urban government will be key to managing the situation, such approaches necessitate broader national strategies that are thoroughly contemplated and structured to provide support for local concerns.

Yet, city managers in Africa—and other regions of the world to varying degrees—control a very small portion of policies with impact at the city level (Stren forthcoming; Mitullah forthcoming). Some authors even argue that cities are so "open" that there is not much policy bite at the city level.[2] Most of what cities need to respond to in the areas of health or education, even in infrastructure, is the prerogative of national policy makers, these authors argue.

Recent research shows that many of the city-level characteristics depend on the performance of local governments (Kaufmann, Léautier, and Mastruzzi 2004). In particular, the ability of local governance to incorporate the voices of its citizens, to establish transparency in the decision-making process, and to combat corruption seem to have an effect upon some city-level qualities. So, there seems to be a possibility for city managers to have an impact. Africa, a region that has not globalized as much as others have, but that has urbanized, provides us with an opportunity to test some of the trade-offs between city-level and national policies.

Comparing the performance in Africa with that of other regions of the world (Table 4.12) and with the averages for the cities in all less-globalized countries (Annex 4.2), we see that Africa does worse on both counts. African cities collect about 10 percent of the revenues of cities in less-globalized countries and spend about half of what these cities spend in capital expenditures per capita. However, African cities have about the same percentage of their budget covering local government wages.

In African cities, one can expect three times more households to be living under the poverty line than the average for cities in less-globalized countries, even though this figure is about the same as in the Arab States and Latin America. So the differences between Africa and the other regions are generally lower than the differences between Africa and the less-globalized cities. This result provides further support for the hypothesis that Africa has urbanized without globalizing and has not seen the benefits of either urbanization or globalization.

Lessons on Globalization and City Performance

The above examination reveals considerable positive linkage between a country's level of globalization and the performance of its cities. It does appear that when a country has higher levels of globalization, its cities are less congested; they offer comparatively more efficient transportation choices, manage waste better, and provide higher levels of education and health outcomes for their citizens. They have relatively better-performing local urban governments. Such cities also deliver higher levels of economic performance and are able to manage poverty more effectively.

While such broad-brush observations may be relevant at the global level, we next attempt to see if similar patterns can be discerned from the data—however limited—on the African countries included in those countries ranked by the A. T. Kearney Globalization Index. We do this after establishing a baseline using the corresponding city-level indicators from the UNCHS database. Table 4.12 compares Africa with other regions of the world, based on UNCHS data. Table 4.13 presents a consolidated picture for four African countries ranked by the Kearney Globalization Index.

Table 4.12. *City-level Performance Indicators across Regions and Country Classifications*

Indicator	Africa	Arab states	Asia Pacific	Latin America	Industrialized countries	Transition economies
City densities, population growth rates, and household sizes						
City densities (persons/ha)	146	252	247	150	82	126
City population growth rates (percent per year)	5	4	3	2	1	declining
Average household size (persons)	6	5	5	4	2	3
Crime in cities						
Murders (per 1,000 city population)	1.49	0.03	0.70	0.63	0.14	0.08
Thefts (per 1,000 city population)	12	2	4	5	54	6
City transportation						
Mean travel time to work (minutes)	37	32	32	37	25	36
Modes of travel to work (percent of total trips to work)						
Private car	12	27	9	26	55	18
Train/tram	0.3	1.7	3.7	1.3	11	29
Bus/minibus	30	30	25	53	13	34
Motorcycle	8	4	19	2	2	2
Bicycle	8	4	15	10	9	2
On foot	37	18	23	16	15	17
Other	9	23	14	5	3	4
City waste management services						
Solid waste generated per capita (tons per year)	0.27	0.28	0.29	0.60	0.51	0.49
Regular waste collection (from percent of city households)	36	65	67	85	99	91
Waste water treated (percent of generated waste water)	15	54	26	18	87	64
Solid waste disposed in open dump (percent of total disposed)	63	32	46	26	1	49

Table 4.12. (Continued)

Indicator	Africa	Arab states	Asia Pacific	Latin America	Industrialized countries	Transition economies
Health and education in cities						
Child mortality (percent of children <5 yrs.)	12	8	5	5	0.4	0.8
Persons per hospital bed	954	410	566	288	132	31
Children per primary classroom	62	42	40	34	23	11
Children per secondary classroom	51	40	40	34	23	11
City government revenue, capital expenditure and wages						
Local government revenue per capita (1993 US$ per year per person)	15	1682	245	252	2763	237
Local government capital exp. per capita (1993 US$ per year per person)	10	32	234	100	1133	77
Wages in the local government budget (percent)	42	59	41	39	38	16
Economic performance of cities						
City product per capita (1993 US$ per year)	682	2,095	862	225	22,926	2,962
Average per capita income (Quintile 3 per person in US$)	252	894	246	948	9,544	1,395
Informal employment (percent)	56	37	40	30	4	5
Equity in cities						
Households below poverty line (percent)	39	34	21	37	14	11
Income disparity (Quintile 5/Quintile 1)	12	10	10	17	10	8

Source: UNCHS 1998; Foreign Policy 2003.

Table 4.13. *City Indicators for Five African Countries by Level of Globalization*

	Globalization ranking				
	33	36	37	41	43
Indicator	Botswana	Uganda	Nigeria	Senegal	Kenya
City growth rates and household sizes					
City population growth rates					
(percent per year)	8.4	5.2	4.4	4.7	4.8
Average household size (persons)	3.5	4.1	5.5	8.1	3.6
Crime in cities					
Murders (per 1,000 city population)	0.007	0.23	0.02	n.a.	0.05
Thefts (per 1,000 city population)	0.5	2.7	1.1	n.a.	3.7
City transportation					
Mean travel time to work (minutes)	20	26	53	28	29
Modes of travel					
(percent of total to-work trips)					
Private car	15	11	13	8	13
Train/tram	0.0	0.1	0.1	0.0	0.8
Bus/minibus	42	17	51	23	49
Motorcycle	0.0	27	4	n.a.	10
On foot	33	38	14	36	25
Other	7	1.2	12	22	0.4
City waste management services					
Solid waste generated per capita					
(tons per year)	0.01	0.82	0.20	0.17	n.a.
Regular waste collection					
(from percent of city households)	98	27	31	n.a.	44
Waste water treated					
(percent of generated waste water)	95	45	0.5	0.8	45
Solid waste disposed in open dump					
(percent of total disposed waste)	99	60	28	100	n.a.
Health and education					
Child mortality					
(percent of children < 5 yrs.)	4.0	11.2	6.3	15.9	8.2
Persons per hospital bed	140	157	941	1,014	319
Children per primary classroom	48	62	44	72	41
Children per secondary classroom	37	56	54	49	41
City government revenue, capital expenditure and wages					
Local government revenue per capita					
(1993 US$ per year)	250	10	3	9	14
Local government capital exp.					
per capita (1993 US$ per year)	181	10	0.9	2.2	9
Wages in the local government budget					
(percent)	43	21	41	24	80
Economic performance of cities					
City product per capita					
(1993 US$ per year)	594	317	57	620	1,147
Avg. per capita income					
(Quintile 3 per person in US$)	n.a.	n.a.	47	159	n.a.
Informal employment (percent)	45	56	72	62	41
Equity in cities					
Households below poverty line (percent)	21	66	63	26	27
Income disparity (Quintile 5/Quintile 1)	n.a.	n.a.	23.44	17.09	n.a.

Source: UNCHS 1998, Global Urban Indicators; *Foreign Policy* 2003.

Allowing for the limited nature of the data on cities, it may be possible to generalize that cities of smaller countries, such as Botswana, may benefit from the country's globalization. This is consistent with an observation by the A. T. Kearney team, which states that small countries tend to have an advantage over larger countries at similar levels of per capita income in the globalization index (*Foreign Policy* 2003).

As an additional source, we draw on work by Gavin Mclachlan, who studies the Port Elizabeth Metropolitan Area in South Africa (Mclachlan 2001). This area in many ways typifies the impact of globalization on the cities of the African region. Mclachlan summarizes this impact as follows:

- The global economy has generated enormous pressure on the economy of the South African city by forcing businesses to become globally competitive. Coastal cities may be benefiting more from this trend than South Africa's inland cities.
- Social and cultural globalization has increased the pressure on traditional societies and culture, making even more difficult the process of urbanization for the African rural poor.
- Globalization has diminished the ability of politicians to respond to pressures experienced by the people and has made it easier for those with means to live outside the immediate control of the state.
- The physical impact of globalization has been to hasten the growth of South Africa's largest cities (Johannesburg/Pretoria, Durban/Pietermaritzburg, Cape Town/Stellenbosch, and Port Elizabeth/Uitenhage) into urban regions.

In addition, it is possible that even when African countries are not highly globalized (Senegal and Kenya are good examples), their cities may benefit from playing a heightened role as important hubs of economic activities within their own countries.

Botswana, which is Africa's most globalized country, has better performance in its principal city, Gaborone, than do any of the other cities included in Table 4.13. Botswana has a very high urbanization rate—almost twice that of cities in Uganda, Nigeria, Senegal, and Kenya—but has smaller household sizes. Gaborone has lower crime rates, performs better in transportation and waste services, and does well on all other indicators. The only exception is city product per capita, which is higher in cities in Kenya and Senegal.

In general, the trends seen in Annex 4.2 do not hold for Africa, with the exception of Botswana. Instead, the patterns vary. In some cases, city performance profiles are better in less-globalized countries; in other cases, the opposite is true. For instance, compare the indicators of performance where cities have less control—city growth rates, city product per capita, and households below the poverty line. There seems to be much better performance for these indicators in Kenya than in Uganda and Nigeria. However, when it comes to the indicators where we expect more control at the city level, we see that there is no clear pattern. This result supports the hypothesis that the capability of city managers to influence city performance makes a difference over and above the pressures of globalization that push cities to perform better. It also provides some support for the hypothesis that there can be well-performing local cities that are less globalized—whose performance is influenced by the role that the city managers play. This is seen in city performance aspects such as crime rates, provision of transportation, waste collection, and social services.

Conclusions

We find that in more-globalized countries, cities grow at a slower pace than in less-globalized countries, even as there is a general slowdown in urbanization in all regions of the world. Such trends lead credence to the argument that if a city cannot act as a global player, it needs to rely more on its regional role—serving its hinterland—and hence needs to grow faster to meet the demands of a regional economy. Cities are important at any level of globalization. They are main engines of growth for the rural hinterland in less-globalized countries, key regional players in moderately globalized countries, and as brokers of local and global interests in highly globalized countries. There are transition costs, as countries move toward more globalization, because cities are sometimes not able to manage the balance between the demand for globally needed services such as transportation, and locally needed services such as health and education, as well as social safety nets.

Cities in countries that are beginning to globalize do provide more employment, but originally most of the opportunities are informal. Informal activities get absorbed into the formal economy as cities globalize even further. There is yet another stage, however, at which the pressures of globalization lead once again to the need for an informal economy, even though the long-term pattern is to reduce the dependence on informality. This result could explain why countries that have poor business environments and hence cannot support new company formation and small-scale enterprises in the formal sector do have these entities in the informal sector. The informal sector in turn becomes a dynamic engine of growth that first taps into global opportunities. The garment industry in Bangladesh is a very good example of this phenomenon, as is the leather industry in Africa.

Better attention to areas in which city managers have control, in combination with globalization, particularly when cities exercise autonomy, can be a powerful instrument to better manage the opportunities of globalization. How cities are managed seems to be important in the differential performance of their economies, over and above the opportunities they may have as a result of globalization.

These results point to three main conclusions for Africa. First, Africa should continue to improve the quality of its decentralization efforts, seeking nuanced solutions, with a smart combination of economic and political factors. Second, the benefits of urbanization in Africa can only be tapped if the larger cities, especially coastal areas, play more of a global and/or regional role than a local one. Third, there is a need to improve the quality of the management of cities in Africa, so that they can best balance the tension between offering services that make them attractive to foreign investment and continuing to serve the needs of their residents and their regional economies.

Our policy analysis is complicated by the degree to which there is interdependence between globalization and city performance. Those cities that perform less well are not attractive for further globalization, yet the competitive pressures of globalization are important for improving local governance. While per capita income and the degree of urbanization do play a role, as they explain many of the reasons for the improved performance of cities, we find that there are other factors indicating that cities do have leverage at the local level to improve their performance. Some cities in highly globalized countries, such as those in Eastern Europe—Ukraine is an example—and Africa—Nigeria, for instance—are in places where international investments have not made much of a dent. We suspect that the quality of city governance may be an important explanatory variable in this regard.

Time lag is also an important issue. The impact of globalization is not felt overnight; there is some lag before results show up. A.T. Kearney's data were collected about a decade after the UNCHS city data. The UN data were gathered in 1993, but actually more likely were a result of 1990 census numbers. For this reason, it is difficult to draw conclusions from the data on the impact of globalization on city behavior. Because of these data weaknesses, we can only perform static comparisons. We are able to look at which areas local governments can independently work on to get better performance—such as provision of transportation services, waste collection, health and education services, and control of urban crime—and areas where cities have to rely on national governments to get any improvement in performance—such as generating urbanization patterns, creating employment opportunities, and managing tools to address income inequality.

Finally, the chapter points to the benefits of empirical approaches to testing various hypotheses on globalization and urbanization. The paucity of data in this regard is a key obstacle to effective policy design at the national and subnational level. Efforts to improve the quality of data at the city level would go a long way to addressing this critical policy gap.

Annex 4.1. *Countries Ranked by the A. T. Kearney Index of Globalization*

A. T. Kearney Globalization Index 2003	Globalized countries	Cities
15	Czech Republic	Prague
22	Croatia	Zagreb
23	Hungary	Budapest
25	Slovenia	Koper, Ljubljana, Maribor
27	Slovak Republic	Bratislava
29	Morocco	Rabat
31	Chile	Santiago
32	Poland	Warsaw
33	Botswana	Gaborone
36	Uganda	Jinja, Kampala, Mbale, Mbarara
37	Nigeria	Ibadan, Kano, Lagos, Onitsha
39	Tunisia	Tunis
40	Romania	Bucharest, Tirgoviste
41	Senegal	Dakar, Kaoloack, Mbour, Richard Toll, Tambacounda, Ziguinchor
42	Ukraine	Donetsk
43	Kenya	Kakamega, Kisumu, Mombasa, Nairobi, Nakuru, Nyeri
44	Sri Lanka	Colombo
45	Russian Federation	Kostroma, Moscow, Nizhny Novgorod, Novgorod, Ryazan
46	Egypt	Assiout, Cairo, Gharbeya, Tenth of Ramadan
50	Pakistan	Lahore
51	China	Chengdu, Foshan, Hefei, Qingdao, Shanghai, Zhangjiagang

(Annex 4.1 continued on next page)

Annex 4.1. *(Continued)*

A. T. Kearney Globalization Index 2003	Globalized countries	Cities
52	Philippines	Cebu, Davao, Metro Manila
54	Bangladesh	Chittagong, Dhaka, Tangail
55	Colombia	Bogota
56	India	Bangalore, Bhiwandi, Chennai (Madras), Delhi, Gulbarga, Hubli-Dharbad, Lucknow, Mumbai (Bombay), Mysore, Tumkur, Varanasi
57	Brazil	Brasilia, Curitiba, Recife, Rio de Janeiro
58	Indonesia	Bandung, Banjarmasin, Jakarta, Medan, Semarang, Surabaya
59	Peru	Cajamarca, Lima, Trujillo
60	Venezuela	Valencia
62	Iran	Mashad, Tehran

Source: *Foreign Policy* 2003.

Annex 4.2. *Differences in Performance Profiles of More-globalized and Less-globalized Countries*

Indicator	More globalized	Less globalized	Difference (percent)	Variance
Economic performance				
City product (1993 US$ per year)	3,818	1,175	69	
Average per capita income (Quintile 3 per person in US$)	2,066	377	82	
Informal employment (percent)	32	40	−25	
			42	0.34
City characteristics				
City density (persons/ha)	96	252	−163	
City population growth rates (percent per year)	2	3	−22	
Average household size (persons)	3	5	−48	
			−78	0.57
Equity				
Households below poverty line (percent)	26	27	−3	
Income disparity (Quintile 5/Quintile 1)	7	12	−74	
			−38	0.25
Transportation services				
Mean travel time to work (minutes)	30	35	−19	
Modes of travel to work:				
Private car (percent of total work trips)	25	10	60	
Train/tram (percent of total work trips)	14	7	50	
Bus/mini bus (percent of total work trips)	23	37	−64	
Motorcycle (percent of total work trips)	4	12	−184	
Bicycle (percent of total work trips)	11	7	31	
On foot (percent of total work trips)	24	22	7	
Other (percent of total work trips)	2	13	−603	
			−100	5.63

Annex 4.2. *(Continued)*

Indicator	More globalized	Less globalized	Difference (percent)	Variance
City waste management services				
Solid waste generated (tons per year per person)	0.5	0.4	24	
Regular waste collection (from percent households)	77	68	12	
Waste water treated (percent of generated)	52	68	−32	
Solid waste disposal methods:				
Landfills (percent of total disposed)	28	35	−25	
Incinerator (percent of total disposed)	11	7	35	
Open dump (percent of total disposed)	42	45	−7	
Recycling (percent of total disposed)	8	10	−37	
Other (percent of total disposed)	12	9	18	
			−1	0.07
Health and education services				
Child mortality (percent of children less than 5 years old)	4	6	−44	
Persons per hospital bed	144	528	−266	
Children per primary classroom	38	43	−12	
Children per secondary classroom	36	44	−21	
			−86	1.46
Local government finances				
Local government revenue (1993 US$ per year per person)	266	115	57	
Local government CAPEX (1993 US$ per year per person)	104	22	79	
Wages in local government budget (percent)	21	38	−80	
			19	0.74
Urban crime				
Murders (per thousand population)	0.1	0.6	−693	
Thefts (per thousand population)	14	5	68	
			−313	28.93

Source: Calculated from UNCHS 1998, Urban Indicators, and *Foreign Policy* 2003, A. T. Kearney Globalization Index 2003.

Notes

This chapter has benefited from extensive comments by Tim Campbell and Christine Kessides, both at the World Bank, and by an anonymous reviewer whose comments were invaluable. Research support was provided by Junko Saito, for which we are very grateful.

1. Since the data on globalization are a decade later than the data on city performance, one could assume that these cities have been attractive to globalized activities because they have been well performing. It is difficult to say much about causality with the type of data we have, as most of what we can do is compare static city profiles across the two categories of globalization.

2. Comments made by Tim Campbell and Gregory Ingram, both at the World Bank, in various forums.

References

Campbell, Timothy. 2003. *The Quiet Revolution: Decentralization and the Rise of Political Participation in Latin American Cities.* Pittsburgh, PA: University of Pittsburgh Press.

Dinghem, Severine, and Frannie Léautier. 2005. "Citizens, Merchants, and Mayors: The Main Players in an Evolving System of Governance at the City Level." Submitted to *State and Local Economics: Issues in Development*, Nova Science Publishers, Inc., February 2005.

Fay, M., and C. Opal. 2000. "Urbanization without Growth: A Not-so-uncommon Phenomenon." Policy Research Working Paper 2412. Washington, DC: World Bank.

Foreign Policy. 2003. A. T. Kearney/Foreign Policy Magazine, Globalization Index 2003. On-line at http://www.atkearney.com/main.taf?p=5,4,1,65.

Kaufmann, Daniel, Frannie Léautier, and Massimo Mastruzzi. 2004. "An Empirical Exploration into Global Determinants of Urban Performance." World Bank Institute Working Papers and Articles (Discussion Paper).Washington, DC: World Bank. On-line at http:/www.worldbank.org/wbi/governance/pdf/govcity.pdf.

Lo, Fu-Chen, and Yue-Man Yeung, eds. 1998. *Globalization and the World of Large Cities.* Tokyo: United Nations University Press.

Mclachlan, Gavin. 2001. "The Impact of Globalization on the Cities of Southern Africa: A Case Study of Port Elizabeth Metropolitan Area." Port Elizabeth,South Africa: University of Port Elizabeth, Department of Economics. On-line at http://www.isocarp.org/Data/case_studies/cases/cs01_4568/gmpaper.htm.

Mitullah, W. Forthcoming. "Tapping Opportunities in Decentralized Governance and Informal Activities for Urban Development in East African Countries." World Bank Institute study. Washington: World Bank.

Rakodi, Carole, ed. 1997. *The Urban Challenge in Africa: Growth and Management of its Large Cities* Tokyo: United Nations University Press.

Simon, D. 1997. "Urbanization, globalization and economic crisis in Africa," Pages 74-109 in *The Urban Challenge in Africa: Growth and Management of Its Large Cities*, ed. by Carole Rakodi. Tokyo: United Nations University Press.

Stren, R. Forthcoming. "An Urbanizing Africa: The Challenge of Informality." World Bank Institute study. Washington: World Bank.

UN 2000. *World Population Prospects: The 2000 Revision,* vol. 1, Comprehensive Tables. New York.

UNCHS (United Nations Commission on Human Settlements). 1998. Global Urban Indicators Database. On-line at http://www.unhabitat.org/programmes/guo/guo_indicators.asp.

UNDESA (United Nations Department of Economic and Social Affairs). 2004. *World Urbanization Prospects: The 2003 Revision.* New York.

5

Explaining Urban Performance: Globalization and Governance

Frannie Léautier and Séverine Dinghem

The role of cities in a globalized world, especially the links between local and global decision-making, is a principal theme of this volume, as it is in most discussions of global governance now. Earlier in this volume, we showed through empirically based exploration the key determinants of the performance of cities (Chapter 3; see also Kaufmann, Léautier, and Mastruzzi 2004). In particular, we explored the dynamic pressures from globalization and accountability that result in better performance at the city level. Nonetheless, we left open the question of the direction of causality between governance and globalization: Does better governance lead to more globalization or does more globalization lead to better governance at the city level? In this chapter, we use a dynamic game between three players—the citizen body, an elected mayor, and a firm making decisions to locate in the city—to better understand the dynamics and uncover key aspects of city governance that can guide policies to improve city performance.

We also examine here and in Chapter 6 the links among the quality of local governance, the scale of the municipality, and the performance of utilities, whether they be water, electricity, garbage collection, or sewerage services. Municipal scale is an increasingly important consideration as demand rises for the universal delivery of utility services; previously, utilities were provided only to populations with a density high enough to justify economically the minimum investments required. (For further discussion of the link between utilities and local governance, see Estache and Kouassi 2002.)

A History of City Governance and Current Trends

As a starting point for our dynamic game, we look at the historical interactions among citizens, mayors, and firms. With that background, we can see current trends and verify and illustrate our conclusions with empirical examples.

The Constitution of Cities

The city is a relatively recent form of social organization. Records of the first large cities only date back to 3,500–4,000 BC in Mesopotamia, and the earliest cities, such as Jericho in 7000 BC, are known to have grown from villages (see Chase-Dunn and Willard 1993; Hamblin 1977; Huot and others 1990; and Escobar and Hodgson 1998). Although these settlements initially depended on subsistence agriculture and domesticated animals, as the civilizations grew in size and trade routes grew in number, these settlements became centers for merchants, craftspeople, traders, and government officials. The division between urban and rural had begun.

The need for organized governance had also begun. The construction of aqueducts, storage tanks, and water distribution systems has been documented as early as 2000 BC in Qumrân. The technologies involved during this period had already been used in Jericho by the Hashmodean kings and were the first documented evidence of a municipal authority providing services to a community. Earlier use of utility services, such as the network designed by the engineers of Herod the Great, were aimed at providing water to a single residence: the king's winter palace (Paul 2000, pp. 114–16).

By the time of the Industrial Revolution in Europe, the number and population of cities multiplied, as large numbers of rural people moved into cities to work for wages in factories. This period is characterized by the empowerment of city representatives, whereby cities gained regional and feudal independence to establish a more direct relationship to existing central governments. In France, municipalities became the basis of administrative organization and are still particularly numerous.[1]

According to Chandler (1987), who provides an excellent history of urban growth in the past 4,000 years, cities have moved in and out of the top 100 list. Memphis in Egypt, with a population of over 30,000 in 3100 BC, held the record of being the largest known city in history for almost 900 years. Memphis was replaced by a series of Babylonian cities, starting with Akkad in what is now modern Iraq.

However, the largest and fastest growth in the world's urban population has taken place in the decades since 1950. The largest city in 1950 was New York, with a population of more than 12 million people. Fifteen years later, in 1965, New York was replaced at the top by Tokyo, with a population of over 20 million (Chandler 1987). The largest city in 2005 in terms of population from the last census is Seoul, South Korea with a population of over 10 million (City Mayors 2003). The largest urban area is still New York, with a population of over 21 million.[2]

Cities today are much smaller than the largest urban populations attained in the past 4,000 years, but they are more interconnected to each other as a result of globalization and more connected to the rural hinterland as a result of commercial and economic ties. Globalization, as measured by the interconnectedness of economies, contributed to the fast pace of urbanization. Today more than half the world's population is urbanized, and megacities in the developing world far surpass the scale of Western cities that grew up in the Industrial Revolution.

Governance at the Local Scale

As cities grew, they needed more and better organization and management for trade, religious activity, defense, transport, communications, and government (Chandler 1987 and more recently United Nations CyberSchoolbus 1996). A number of authors have looked at the performance of cities throughout history. De Long and Shleifer (1992), for example, looked at European cities from 1000 to 1800, comparing their economic performance as a function of their political regime. They found that cities that were ruled by princes—which they assumed to be badly governed, usually centralized regimes with extortionist tax structures—performed worse than cities, such as Venice, Florence, or Amsterdam, which were ruled by merchants or parliaments. De Long and Schleifer argued that princes seek to maximize influence and revenue and prevent other regimes from coming up, while merchants seek to maintain and expand the flow of commerce, and parliaments seek to limit tax burdens and maximize economic growth. Our chapter demonstrates that, in the dynamic interactions between a citizen (representing the parliamentary position in De Long and Schleifer's analysis), a mayor (representing De Long and Schleifer's prince), and a firm (representing De Long and Schleifer's merchant), we can expect different balances to be struck among interests, depending on the type of mayor. This is an insight we will revisit in the next sections.

A study by Rauch (1995) looked at the performance of cities in the United States during the Progressive Era, which covers roughly the first two decades of the twentieth century. During this period, there was a wave of municipal reforms, which transformed the governments of many American cities. These reforms were intended to improve performance, since the political model of city management was not leading to the expected results. Rauch found that when cities are managed by Weberian institutional structures, meaning that there is a professional civil service that is responsible for the activities of city management, as opposed to predatory ones where the mayor rules totally, they make decisions to allocate resources for longer-term gains, such as investments in infrastructure. The evolution of a Weberian structure or "professional bureaucracy" at the city level to ensure improved performance in the provision of services to citizens is of keen interest to us, as it is a measure of the degree to which a city is governable (see Chapter 2 for the definition of governance).

Henderson and Venables (2004) developed a model of the dynamics of city formation in countries where the urban population is growing steadily. They considered the forward-looking behavior of city managers in the specification of investments in housing and urban infrastructure assets. Henderson and Venables compared the effects on city performance of governance measures versus financial constraints, where performance is related to the efficient size of cities. Their results on the role of governance are of particular interest to us.[3]

The Mayor

The office of the mayor has existed since the fifth century in some cities and has changed dramatically over the years (Royal Borough of Kingston upon Thames 2005). In the Middle Ages, the mayor was acknowledged as the "first citizen" of the town and had a council to assist him. He also was the custodian of peace and presided over civil and criminal courts. Mayoral powers at the time included: (a) power to regulate the private sector such as ensuring the size of loaves of bread and seizing bread of unlawful size as well as holding the bakers responsible (Lambarde 1570, 5 Henry V c. 6); (b) power to arrest those disturbing the peace (Lambarde 1570, 2 ED. II c. 3); and (c) power to compel persons to go into service, and to deal with labor issues such as matters relating to servants and apprentices (Lambarde 1570, 5 Eliz. I c. 4).

Over time, the role of the mayor has evolved to include a legally recognized role within a national setting, with well-developed political and civic responsibilities. The degree of regulation of mayoral activity varies across cities and countries, as does the relationship between mayors, citizens, and firms. The power of the mayor in Common Law countries has been tremendously reduced since medieval times, and today's mayor in such countries does not have as much power as a mayor in fifteenth-century Europe. In Roman Law countries, especially the ones that introduced prerogatives to decentralize central government functions, mayors have gained financial and political independence. Moreover, there has been a revolution in the degree to which citizens participate in choosing mayors in both Common Law and Roman Law countries. A history of interactions between citizens, merchants, and mayors has lead to this evolution, all pushing toward improved governance and better delivery of services.

A study by the French National Institute for Statistical and Economic Studies (INSEE) used France as a case study to show the shifting importance of the mayor's role in local governance (Besson 2002). In France, the mayor's role has shifted from being a representative of the state—as he was not elected but nominated by the central government until 1848—to being a local representative, with a large degree of autonomy and a local budget, since the beginning of the decentralization process of 1982. Following the decentralization laws of 1982, 1983, and 1986, the volume of investments carried out by municipalities increased by 14.9 percent in 1988. Between 1978 and 1993, the local investments in education and schools went up by 7.5 percent. By contrast, the share of direct municipal investment in infrastructure has decreased by 11.2 percent as the municipalities delegated public infrastructure services to the private sector. This privatization helped to reduce the debt burden of local administrations, which decreased from 9 percent to 7.5 percent of the gross national income. The INSEE study also showed that the volume of investments made by a municipality is strongly influenced by the electoral cycle.

Modeling the Interactions of Citizens, Mayors, and Firms

This section develops a model of the interactions among three main players who are key to the city's development. We define the city as a geographically bounded space where interactions take place between citizens, a mayor (or municipal authority), and private firms, as the main actors of the local economy. We observe the outcomes of these interactions as the performance of a city, meaning the ability of the city to provide (a) a good quality of life, which is of interest to the citizens; (b) a good business address with access to markets or quality services, which is of interest to the firm; and (c) a well-governed place with the resources and political support needed to continue to improve quality of life and offer good services, which is of interest to the mayor. We develop a model for the general case of interactions among the three players and expand from it with special cases.

The General Case

To model this process, we start the game off with a citizen in a city that has an existing endowment of quality of life and quality of governance. We denote a city type by h^t, which represents a history of performances of the city over a time period t. When looking at a collection of cities from the outside, a city type would be an observation from a feasible set of city types $H = \{h^0, h^1, \dots, h^T\}$.

All players (citizen, mayor, and firm) observe $h^t = a^0, a^1, \dots, a^{t-1}$ for all $t \geq 1$, as h^t comes from realized choices of actions at all time periods before t. In such a specification, we assume that the actions a^t of the players create the city performance profile h^t.

For the purposes of this chapter, we use the Hirschmann (1970) framework to derive the actions of the citizens and their message-bearing content to the mayor.

Hirschmann's framework assumes that citizens seek to maximize their utility, through three options:

- *Exit,* if they are not happy with the quality of life offered by the city, by physically leaving the city or by seeking alternative sources of service, including self-provision.
- Be *loyal* to the city and stay, consuming services offered by the municipality.
- Use *voice* to vote the mayor out of office or lodge complaints to the municipality and get services fixed.

The mayor observes the citizen's choice and responds in several possible ways:

- *Ignore* the demands and preferences of the citizens.
- *Satisfy* them by responding to the demands of the citizens.

A municipality that functions on a Weberian basis would have a mayor that relies on a council broadly representing the views of citizens. Other types of governance arrangements would be more political and respond to shorter-term benefits, such as the mayor's reelection or personal gain, as was identified by Rauch (1994). Our model follows the Weberian-Rauch principle that cities governed under more participatory arrangements tend to advance the common good by making long-term investments in city services.

A firm observes the outcome of the choices of citizens and mayors and chooses its response. We look at a firm that is seeking to invest in a city outside of its headquarters. Such a firm has three options based on the observed information about the city:

- *Exit,* by not locating in the city or, if there, deciding to leave.
- *Locate* and conduct transparent business in the city
- Locate and seek to *influence* the local politics through bribes, state capture, and other forms of influence.

Citizens, mayors, and firms discount future utilities using a discount factor $\partial > 1$. The discount factor $\partial = e^{-r\Delta}$, where r is the rate of time preference and Δ is the period length (a normal period to consider being the electoral cycle for a mayor which is about five years).

The utility for a citizen i is:

$$U_i = E_\sigma (1-\partial) \sum_{t=0}^{\infty} (\partial^t g_i * \sigma^t(h^t)) \tag{1}$$

where E_σ is the expectation with respect to the distribution over infinite histories of city performance that is generated by a strategy profile σ. We denote the null history by h^0, to represent a new city where residents have just moved in or where a new mayor has just been elected. The citizen's message to the mayor, which is represented by the series of choices the citizen makes, influence the utility of the citizen, and the citizen is impacted by the real quality of life of the city, the response of the mayor to their messages, and the choices made by firms. We use the convention (U_i, S_i, σ_i) for the utility, strategy, and choices of the citizens, respectively, for the whole game, and (g_i, a_i, σ_i) for the stage game building block for a repeated game, which is the subgame component of a repeated game.

The utility expressions for the mayor and for the firm have a similar form, with notation j for the mayor and k for the firm. The theorem is detailed in Annex 5.1.

With such a structure, we define the payoff structure for the citizen as:

$$\underline{v_i} = \text{exit} \; ; \; \underline{v_i} + \theta = \text{voice; and } v_i = \text{loyal}$$

The payoff structure for the firm is:

$$\underline{v_k} = \text{exit}; \; \underline{v_k} = \text{influence; and } v_k = \text{locate}$$

And the payoff structure for the mayor[4] is:

$$\underline{v_j} = \text{ignore citizen}; \; v_j + \theta = \text{ignore firm; and } v_j = \text{satisfy citizen and firm.}$$

These strategies are a Nash Equilibrium for any $T > R.I$ and for $T > R.I$ $(\max_a g_i(a) - \underline{v_i})/\varepsilon$ the average payoffs are within 2ε of v where R denotes a repeated cycle (Benoit and Krishna 1985).

When facing a reelection, the mayor will play "satisfy" in *T-1* at the minimum, to ensure citizens play "loyal" at *T*. A firm will either "exit" or "locate," if play by the mayor is "satisfy," within a well-governed system. But the firm can also play "influence" at *T-2*, if the mayor has no chance of getting "loyal" from citizens (in a situation where it is the mayor's last term in service for instance). If a firm plays "influence" and the mayor can provide some services to the firm, then it is a worthwhile strategy for the mayor and the firm at period *T-2*.

Global and Local Cities within a Responsive Governance Framework

In this section, the definitions of a global city and a local city refer to a framework developed in Chapter 3 and in Kaufmann, Léautier, and Mastruzzi (2004). A global city is one that is connected to activities in other countries through trade, finance, and intense communication (telephone, internet, tourist travel), while a local city is one that has minimal interactions with other cities, but does serve as a regional or urban-rural center.

The pattern of choices that comes from a game such as the one developed in the previous section can be classified into the following main types of results.

The Case of a Global City

A global city that is well performing and well governed would have an end state that comes from a mapping of the three players' interactions in the form of (citizens' choice, mayor's position, firm's strategy), as follows:

(loyal/voice, *satisfy firm*, locate) → (loyal/voice, *satisfy citizen*, locate).

A global city that is well governed but poorly performing would have an end state that comes from a mapping of:

(voice, *ignore firm*, locate) → (voice, *satisfy citizen*, locate/exit).

A global city, with state capture or other forms of influence, would have an end state that comes from a mapping of:

(loyal, *ignore citizen*, influence) → (loyal, *satisfy firm*, locate).

A global city can become a local city that is well governed and well performing, with an end state that comes from a mapping of:

(loyal/voice, *ignore firm*, influence) → (loyal/voice, *satisfy citizen*, exit).

This means that the city was able to attract some firms at earlier time periods (perhaps through perfectly legitimate reasons) and does well to meet the needs of its local residents, but cannot attract companies to locate there permanently. However, such a city is not responsive to negative influence, such as bribery or state capture, and hence is a well-governed local city, with little interest to outside firms.

The Case of a Local City

A local city that is well governed but poorly performing, such that no companies locate there and the citizens have to provide their own services or do with poor performance, would have an end state that comes from a mapping like:

(voice, *ignore firm*, influence) → (voice, *satisfy citizen*, exit).

A poorly governed and poorly performing local city, where the residents are not getting the services they need and are also not able to get a response from their mayor to their concerns, would have an end state that comes from a mapping of:

(voice, *ignore firm*, exit) → (loyal/voice, *ignore citizen*, exit).

Generalizing from these mappings, we can say that an observed outcome of a set of actions taken by a citizen, mayor, and firm would represent a distinct strategy path. That path defines the city type h^{t+1}, which we would evolve into the set $H = \{h^0, h^1, \ldots, h^T\}$ where $H = T(a_i, a_j, a_k)$. The observer of a data set that is an outcome of such strategic choices would see a city type h^t with probability $p(h^t)$, where $p(h^t) > 0$ for every T and $p(h^0) + p(h^1) + \ldots + p(h^T) = 1$.

The general form of the payoff function for the mayor is $U_j(a_i, a_j, a_k)$ since the mayor has to respond to the messages from citizens and the strategic choices of firms, but is also influenced by the history of his responses. Such responses could include having been re-elected because he made citizens happy, having had to respond to unsatisfied citizens who complained, or having had to deal with firms that left the city for other locations or decided not to locate in the city. A special case of the mayor who ignores messages from the citizens—representing a bad governance framework—would have a response that is based on the following utility function, since the mayor will ignore the message sent by the citizen:

$$\text{Max} \sum p(h^t)U_j(h^t, a_j, a_k) \tag{2}$$

The payoff for the firm is $U_k(h^t, a_j)$ which depends on the real quality-of-life profile of the city—rather than the message from citizens to their mayor—and the response of the mayor. We will look at a special case where the mayor sends information to the firm to signal good governance and a good business address.

Using the payoff structure developed in the last section we see that the mapping (loyal, satisfy firm, locate) is superior to the mapping (voice, ignore firm, influence) that in turn is superior to (exit, ignore firm, exit). We can express this as:

$$(v_i + v_j + v_k) > \{(v_i + \theta) + (v_j + \varphi) + (v_k + \varepsilon)\} > (\underline{v_i} + \underline{v_j} + \underline{v_k}) \tag{3}$$

A Special Case When the Mayor's Action Is Not Observed

We look at a special case where the citizen takes the lead action and the firm is an observer. This case would be relevant for multinational firms making decisions to locate in a given city. In such a case, the mayor's action is not observed. The firm

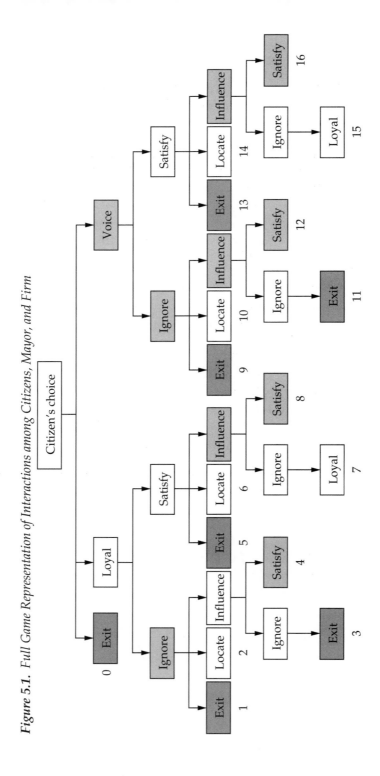

Figure 5.1. Full Game Representation of Interactions among Citizens, Mayor, and Firm

looks to see whether the citizen is "loyal" and deduces that the mayor could have played "satisfy citizen," which is the expected response in a well-governed framework. If the firm observes that the citizen has used "voice," it can deduce that this is an indication that the mayor can be "influenced." Such a special case would be relevant to an outside firm that is looking at imperfect information. Such a firm would have access to public information, such as "Mayor X has been reelected to a second term" or "Citizens of City Y have demonstrated against the mayor for poor garbage collection." The actions of citizens can convey information to firms.

We develop an extensive form of this game (Gibbons 1992), which is shown in Figure 5.1. For simplicity, we do not include the payoff structure in the figure.

From Figure 5.1, we see that there are 17 distinct outcomes that result from this game, labeled from 0 to 16. Some outcomes (shown in light shading) lead to an end state of corrupt cities that may perform poorly for their citizens, but well for the firms (4 and 12), or well for their citizens and firms, but firms have influence over the mayors (8 and 16) and have captured them. While other outcomes (no shading) lead to an end state of well-performing and well-governed cities (6, 7, 14, and 15). Other outcomes, which are shown in dark shading, lead firms to exit after receiving more information (3 and 11) or to decide not to come on the basis of existing information (1, 5, 9, and 13). One outcome (0) leads to no city at all as the citizens exit. Henderson and Venables (2004) also find the conditions under which such a result can be obtained, using a different specification of a dynamic model with forward-looking behavior.

In such a game, the outcome at the city level of strategies 1, 3, 5, 9, 11, and 13 would be to have no foreign companies investing in the city. We called such cities "local" in the definition employed in Kaufmann, Léautier, and Mastruzzi (2004) and also in the discussion in the last section. A well-governed and well-performing local city would be represented by outcome 3 and 11, where, despite having the mayor responsive to citizens needs, companies decided not to locate there, for reasons other than governance. A poorly governed global city would be represented by the outcomes from strategies 4, 8, 12, and 16.

Let us look now at the payoff functions of some of the subgames. At the first stage of the game, or in a subgame where we observe the citizen, we would have an extended form as shown in Figure 5.2.

The history of the subgame in Figure 5.2 would be visible in the performance of the city at the end of the game, which would be unique to a particular mapping, and a function of the payoff structure. We represent such performance as a simple

Figure 5.2. *Subgame Representation of Citizen and Mayor's Choices in Stage 1*

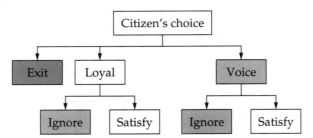

sum of the payoffs of the three players at the end of that stage. The city performance for the respective paths would be:

Map 0: Citizen "exit" at the first stage: v_i

Map (1, 2, 3, 4): Citizen "loyal" followed by "ignore" by mayor: $(v_i + \underline{v_j})$

Map (5, 6, 7, 8): Citizen "loyal" followed by "satisfy" by mayor: $(v_i + v_j)$

Map (9, 10, 11, 12): Citizen "voice" followed by "ignore" by mayor: $\{(\underline{v_i} + \theta) + \underline{v_j}\}$

Map (13, 14, 15, 16): Citizen "voice" followed by "satisfy" by mayor: $\{(\underline{v_i} + \theta) + v_j\}$

From this subgame, we can see that the mappings have the following ranking in terms of city performance, if θ is small:

$$(v_i + v_j) > \{(\underline{v_i} + v_j) + \theta\} > (v_i + \underline{v_j}) > \{(\underline{v_i} + \underline{v_j}) + \theta\} > v_i \qquad (4)$$

The superiority of good governance—that is, when a mayor is responsive to citizens—is shown in that Map (13, 14, 15, 16) is superior to Map (1, 2, 3, 4). But it is possible for the mayor to hedge and ignore the citizen in this first stage, since Map (9, 10, 11, 12) is superior to Map (5, 6, 7, 8), and the mayor can also be proactive and respond to citizens' needs before they voice concerns, since Map (13, 14, 15, 16) has the best possible city performance.

With such a subgame, we can now look more carefully at the stage where we introduce the firm's choices. Since the firm is an observer and would have seen the city performance history, we would have one simple choice. If citizens are exiting, then a rational firm would exit as well. We do not develop Map 0 any further. We explore the other maps in more detail to see why a poor governance framework would be superior to a good governance framework in the first stage. This is shown in Figures 5.3 and 5.4.

Map 1 at Stage 2 is the outcome of (loyal, ignore, exit): $(v_i + \underline{v_j} + v_k)$

Map 2 at Stage 2 is the outcome of (loyal, ignore, locate): $(v_i + v_j) + \underline{v_k}$

Map (3, 4) at Stage 2 is the outcome of (loyal, ignore, influence): $\{(v_i + \underline{v_j}) + v_k + \varepsilon\}$

With ε being small, we see that Map 2 is superior to Maps 1 and (3, 4), and even in stage 2 of the game, there is still a preference for a bad governance framework, where the mayor ignores the citizens whose loyalty she has, and firms choose to

Figure 5.3. *Subgame Representation of Citizen, Mayor, and Firm's Choices in a Poor Governance Framework with Citizen Loyalty*

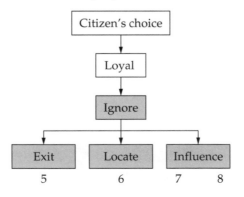

Figure 5.4. *Subgame Representation of Citizen, Mayor, and Firm's Choices in a Poor Governance Framework with Citizen Voice*

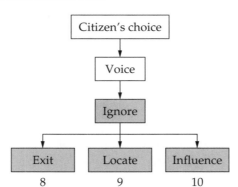

locate there, without at first influencing the mayor. This is possibly due to imperfect information at this stage. We do not know if the citizen is loyal to the mayor because the mayor delivers good services or because the citizens are apathetic.

We also look at the special case of "voice," which we develop in the subgame in Figure 5.4. City performance at stage 2 following a "voice" play by a citizen is shown below:

Map 9 at Stage 2 is the outcome of (voice, ignore, exit): $\{(\underline{v}_i + \theta) + \underline{v}_j + \underline{v}_k\}$

Map 10 at Stage 2 is the outcome of (voice, ignore, locate): $\{(\underline{v}_i + \theta) + \underline{v}_j + \underline{v}_k\}$

Map (11, 12) at Stage 2 is the outcome of (voice, ignore, influence):
$\{(\underline{v}_i + \theta) + \underline{v}_j) + (\underline{v}_k + \varepsilon)\}$

Comparing Map (3, 4) to Map (11, 12), we see that the city performance, as represented by the total payoff structure at the end of stage 3 of the game, is poorer when "influence" by the firm follows a map of (loyal, ignore) than when "influence" by the firm follows a map of (voice, ignore). This result shows that citizen voice counts as a deterrent to bad governance, even if firms try to influence the mayor and we are not yet certain of the mayor's choice n the following stage of the game. The beginnings of good governance creeping into city performance can be seen at the end of stage 3 of the game.

Using the terminal states only, we can derive the following conditions for influence and their governance implications. A poorly performing but well-governed city would be one with the following mapping structure: (voice, satisfy citizen, influence, satisfy firm, voice, satisfy citizen). A well-performing, but poorly governed city (such as with state capture) would be one with a mapping of: (voice, satisfy citizen, influence, satisfy firm, loyal, satisfy citizen). As long as the mayor gives the citizens what they need, even if she receives bribes from firms, the city will be well performing, and firms and citizens will stay.

The analysis in this section provides us with sufficient impetus to see if there is empirical proof of the dominance of good governance in the context of globalization. From the analysis, we should expect good governance to interact positively with globalization—having firms locating in a city—but also to have less impact when citizens and firms have options for exit, such as when they can self-provide a service like telephones or electricity. We also should expect a (∪-shaped curve when comparing city size and city performance. This is because well-performing cities that are small could be small because they have a framework of governance that does not allow influence by firms. If a medium city is badly governed, it would eventually lose citizens and company activity and hence would shrink in size. For a medium size city to grow, it would have to be well governed. In such a simple framework, medium-size cities should have the worst performance. An empirical test of this result indeed shows that this is the case, as can be seen in the following section.

Empirical Evidence Based on City Characteristics

To test the theoretical framework in Figures 5.1 through 5.4 using empirical evidence, we employ a data set that has been constructed from various sources. These data were used extensively in Chapter 3 and in Kaufmann, Léautier, and Mastruzzi (2004), and we refer to specific results in this chapter for which the theoretical framework offers additional proof. We look at four types of data from an observation of city histories: (a) the quality of life as experienced by a citizen; (b) the observed quality of governance of the city; (c) the observed pattern of firms' decisions to locate in a city; and (d) the type of information firms would have access to before making a decision to locate in a city.

For measures of what a citizen would be looking for, we use a quality-of-life index developed by Mercer Human Resource Consulting (2002), which is a database of survey data from 215 cities with assessments and evaluations of 39 key quality-of-life determinants, grouped in the following categories: political and social environment, economic environment, socio-cultural environment, medical and health considerations, schools and education, public services and transportation, recreation, consumer goods, housing, and natural environment. In this database, New York City has an index of 100. Zurich has the highest quality of life, and Brazzaville has the lowest.

For the quality of governance by the mayor, we use three indicators derived from various sources including: control of corruption, bribery in utility, and state capture. These indicators are developed in detail in Kaufmann, Kraay, and Mastruzzi (2004).

For the decision by the firm to locate in the city, we use data from Taylor and Walker (2004), which is a database that measures the number of offices of major advertising, accounting, and financial firms in each city for 161 cities in 114 countries. We also use data from other sources, such as the A.T. Kearney Index of Globalization (*Foreign Policy* 2002), which we use as a proxy for stable dynamics when firms have chosen to locate and stay in a city. The globalization index builds on indicators of trade, finance, personal contact, and information exchange.

For the type of information a firm may have about a city before its decision to locate there, we use city-level indicators constructed through internet searches of (a) what the city's population is, (b) whether the city has a website, (c) whether information on city budgets and business regulations are available on such websites, (d) whether the city is the country's capital (for political influence), and (e) whether the city is a port (for ease of export).

We find evidence that strategies 3, 7, 11, and 15 are superior to strategies 4, 8, 12, and 16, as shown in Figure 5.1. In other words, the positive dynamics of interaction between the citizen's push for local accountability and firm's push to get influence,

Figure 5.5. *Indicators of Good Governance on Bribery and Crime in Local and Global Cities*

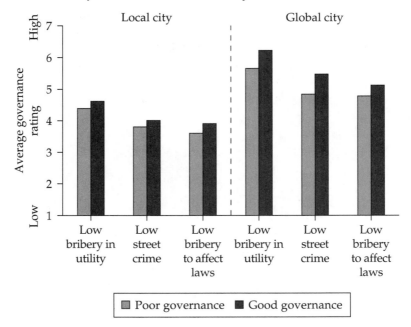

Sources: Kaufmann and Kraay 2002; Kaufmann, Léautier, and Mastruzzi 2004; and World Economic Forum 2003.

but within a well-functioning municipal governance in a globalized world, are evident when you look at the fact that global cities achieve higher governance ratings than local cities, as shown in Figure 5.5. Global cities are better governed than local cities, because the added pressure by firms for good governance, in addition to the pressure by citizens, makes a difference. We also see that country-level globalization (using the Kearney composite) is superior to city-level globalization (using the Taylor index), but this difference is more profound for global cities than for local cities.[5] This result is evidence that the interaction across many cities and many firms leads to better governance outcomes than within a single city.

Furthermore, when firms try to influence city mayors, evidence suggests that the firms do not increase their long-run capability to stay in the city and perform (that is, the firm's behavior eventually leads to exit and hence lower levels of globalization), as shown in Figure 5.6. We see that high globalization is strongly associated with high governance at the city level for variables such as illegal party financing, diversion of public funds, or the quality of the postal system.

There is strong evidence that when mayors satisfy the needs of their citizens and are not corrupt and influenced by firms, the quality of life is good (Figure 5.7).

But quality of life is not always better when cities are more globalized, as can be seen Figure 5.8, where there is a lot of variation between the quality of life achieved and the level of globalization. The analysis in Figure 5.8 is based on a comparison of the degree of city-level globalization (as measured by the number of international firms located in the city from the Taylor 2001 data set) and the quality of life faced by the average citizen (taken from the Mercer 2004 index of quality of life). We used only the top 50 cities ranked by quality of life to do the analysis. The assumption was that cities that are better managed (with good governance) would

Figure 5.6. *Indicators of Good Governance on Finance and Communication Services in Local and Global Cities*

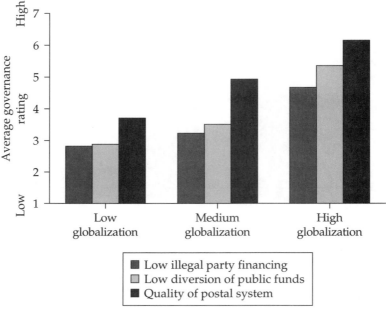

Source: World Economic Forum 2003.

Figure 5.7. *Relationship between Quality of Life and Corruption at the City Level*

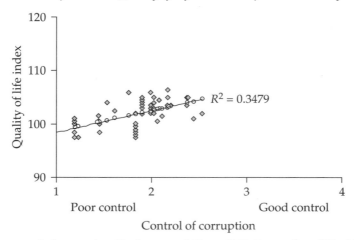

Source: For control of corruption: Kaufmann and Kraay 2004. For quality of life: Mercer Human Resource Consulting 2004. Mercer's survey provides an evaluation of quality of life in 215 cities. We have used the 50 cities with the highest ranking in quality of life to catch the maximum effect of the corruption variable. The Mercer study is based on detailed assessments and evaluations of 39 key quality-of-life determinants, grouped in the following categories: political and social environment; economic environment; sociocultural environment; medical and health considerations; schools and education; public services and transportation; recreation; consumer goods; housing; and natural environment. In Mercer's Quality of Life Index: New York City = 100 (Zurich ranks highest, Brazzaville lowest).

Figure 5.8. *Relationship between Quality of Life and Globalization at the City Level*

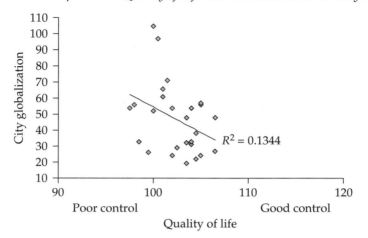

Source: For Control of Corruption: Kaufmann and Kraay 2004. Globaliization data taken from Taylor 2001. Globalization is defined as the number of international firms located in the city, based on 46 "global" advanced producer service firms in 55 world cities. Global firms are defined as having offices in at least 15 different cities. The analysis is done using the cities in the top 50 of the quality-of-life ranking according to Mercer Human Resource Consulting 2004. An analysis done using 261 cities from the Kaufmann-Léautier-Mastruzzi database indicates that when more cities are included the regression line is positive and significant, with good governance contributing to more globalization.

attract more firms to locate there, up to a point where the presence of firms may result in a deterioration in the quality of life.

This evidence suggests that the added pressure from firms to improve performance does have an influence on the outcome of city performance. It also suggests that citizen pressures to keep quality of life high may also act as deterrents to firms locating in such cities.[6]

The results in Figures 5.7 and 5.8 and a more detailed econometric analysis show that the theoretical framework developed earlier in this chapter does indeed have merit when looking at the dynamics of choices made by citizens and firms at the city level. We see that whether a city has a website makes a difference in the quality of its governance, which is of interest both to its citizens and to firms locating there. But whether the city's website has the information a firm needs to set up a business is much more important as a variable in explaining the differential performance of cities across a number of key indicators of governance. Whether a city is global or not also matters. In this analysis, the definition of a global city is based on the number of firms that have located in the city.

The importance of prior information to firms also correlates closely with the quality of services provided at the city level, as shown in Table 5.1. Cities with a website have better quality of services than those that do not. Furthermore, in cities where a citizen can get access to information on the budget (a measure of transparency and accountability) or there is information on how to start a business (a measure of good response to firms in a transparent manner), services also tend to be better. These data show that good governance (represented by the "satisfy" response by the mayor to the citizens' "voice") leads to better outcomes at the city level.

Table 5.1. *City Performance and Availability of City Information to Citizens and Firms in the Non-OECD Sample*

City performance indicator	City has a website		Website has information on budget		Website has information on how to start a business	
	No	Yes	No	Yes	No	Yes
Access to sewerage (%)	44	54	46	70	45	72
Access to water (%)	62	68	63	92	62	90
Access to electricity (%)	75	76	75	91	74	93
Access of the population to telephone lines (%)	84	93	86	99	86	95
Overall number of cities	210	58	262	6	256	12

Note: Data are average ratings drawn from the sample of 274 cities in non-OECD countries.

Source: Constructed from data taken from the UNCHS Urban Observatory data on city performance and from a search of the World Wide Web to determine whether a city has a website and what is posted in it. For more detail on the data, see Kaufmann, Léautier, and Mastruzzi (2004).

The French Experience to Improve Local Governance

To illustrate the dynamic interaction of citizens, mayors, and firms, we examine some specific cases involving large water municipal contracts in France. Municipal activities are particularly relevant in France, because the country has the largest number of municipalities for its geographic size and population. There are 36,565 municipalities in France, among which 31,927 villages have less than 2,000 inhabitants. These villages, home to 15 million inhabitants, represent about 25 percent of the population (Figure 5.9).

Context

Decentralization has given greater power and has provided important public resources to local government, transferring key responsibilities for public welfare to management at the level of cantons and regions. Decentralization has also extended opportunities for corruption and given local politicians powers that they are not always able to manage successfully. France has been involved in a transition to a managerial model of public administration, with the opening of previously public functions to private contractors. In the late 1970s, 75 percent of the municipalities in France were managing their water services through *régies municipales*. Twenty years later, 80 percent of the water distribution was managed by the private sector—the number of contracts signed with the municipalities peaked between 1982 and 1992. There has also been a sharp increase in public-private capital companies, which have been the origin of a number of infamous affairs.

Examples of bad governance at the local level

Since the implementation of decentralization law in the 1980s, local politicians have become involved in illicit exchanges related to various practices. Several cases have been disclosed, raising public dissatisfaction and triggering new laws and regula-

Figure 5.9. *Municipalities in France, by Population, 2003*

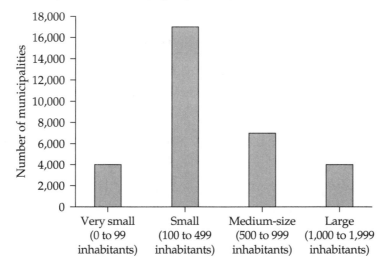

Source: INSEE 1999.

tions to mitigate the risk of bad governance. These cases were built on very different examples of bad governance practices:

- *Lyonnaise des Eaux and Générale des Eaux: questionable competition practices.* In 1980, the two main French water companies, Lyonnaise des Eaux and Générale des Eaux, were each fined FRF 2 million for collusion in the bids for the concession of Versailles, Martinique, and French Guyana.
- *Toulouse: questionable bidding practices.* Fraudulent practices are not the only issue when dealing with public service delegation; unfair measures to competition or to the consumers also provide examples of bad governance. In 1990, CGE paid an entry right of FRF 550 million to the municipality of Toulouse for its water concession. At the same time, CGE inherited a burden of FRF 770 million of debts and liabilities from the previous municipal régie.
- *The Noir-Botton affair: bad governance and mayor's personal profit.* The Noir-Botton Affair (1992–1998) concerned the financing of political campaigns and personal advantages given to the former mayor of Lyon, now dismissed, by his daughter-in-law, who was involved in show business. Benefits included the distribution of gifts to obtain broadcasts and the bankruptcy of a firm providing him with financial resources.
- *Political and elected representatives: opportunities for corruption.* Other scandals involving the financing of political parties at the national and local levels also implicated French private companies and political representatives. In 1984, there were 69 verdicts against political and elected representatives for corruption-related charges; this figure almost doubled by 1987 (which had 133 judgments) and more than doubled again to reach 286 judgments in 1997.
- *The Carignon Affair: bad governance and political party financing.* The Carignon Affair (1996) involved the former mayor of Grenoble, Alain Carignon, who was charged with manipulating competition for public contracts, thereby obtaining personal benefits and financing his political career.

In July 1989, he privatized the municipal water services without a bidding process. By the end of 1995 water prices had increased dramatically from FRF 4.85 to FRF 13.59 (US$0.75 to $2.20 per cubic meter), although the network did not need any major investments or renewals. In 1994, French magistrates found that the water service was privatized in exchange for contributions by Lyonnaise des Eaux to the electoral campaign of Alain Carignon and other gifts totaling over FRF 19 million. They prosecuted Carignon, his main advisor at the city hall, and two executives of Lyonnaise. In 1995 and 1996, they were convicted of paying or receiving bribes and sentenced to prison. The courts also ruled that the consumers could claim compensation of a total of FRF 300,000, because the water company had used fictitious accounting to inflate the price of water charged to consumers. As a consequence, Grenoble water services were partially turned back to the public sector in 1996 and the water tariff dropped by 11 percent. The water company returned fully to the public in 2000.

- *The Boucheron Affair: bad governance for personal gain.* In July 1997, a junior French minister Jean-Michel Boucheron was jailed for two years, with a further two suspended, and fined FRF 1 million for taking bribes from companies bidding in public tender. Boucheron reportedly had received fees of FRF 327,000 for a fictitious job by Générale des Eaux in exchange for giving the utility a water concession in Angoulême. He was also found guilty of taking bribes of FRF 500,000 in 1986–89 from various companies.

Reactions to Bad Governance

These infamous cases triggered public concern about public service delegation to the private sector. Not only were the cases judged in courts of law, but they also initiated legislation and other measures to fight a bad governance practices and outcomes:

- *Law N 92-3, the "Water Law," January 3, 1992.* The Water Law shifted accounting responsibilities to the municipal level and introduced accounting measures aimed at controlling the fair cost-recovery of water services at the municipal level.
- *Law N 92-1282.* This law changed the procedures, in particular the bidding process, to award water concession and water contracts.
- *Law N 93-122, the "Sapin Law," January 29, 1993.* The Sapin Law was passed to prevent corruption and bring more transparency in the public bidding process. The law made it compulsory to adopt competitive bidding for public service delegation contracts and imposed a strict regulatory framework for the content of these contracts.
- *November 18, 1994.* National Water Day, when the Minister of Environment, Michel Barnier, created the National Water Price Observatory.
- *Law N 95-101, the "Barnier Law," February 2, 1995.* The Barnier Law made annual reporting, including a price analysis, compulsory for both municipal and private operators in the water sector, forbid entry rights for bidding, set stricter limits on the duration of contracts, and introduced the

possibility of suing companies and municipalities that did not comply with these requirements.

- *December 19, 1996.* The Direction Générale de la Concurrence, de la Consommation et de la Répression des Fraudes (General Council for Competition, Consumption and Fight against Fraud) published a report on the price of water in France from 1991 to 1996.
- *January 27, 1997.* The Cour des Comptes (National Audit Department) published a report, "The management of water and wastewater services by municipalities," criticizing local governance.
- *August 7, 1998.* The administrative court of Grenoble canceled the city concession renegotiation with Lyonnaise des Eaux, because its did not comply with the competition regulations applicable to public services.
- *December 22, 1999.* The High Council of Public Sector recommended the creation of a water and urban services regulation authority to control the transparency of the water market.
- *July 17, 2002.* The Conseil de la Concurrence (Competition Board) published a report on the water market in France, focusing on the level of competition prevailing in the sector.
- *2002–2004.* Several major water concessions were terminated and rebid. The water tariffs have significantly decreased in several large municipalities in France.

These historical illustrations provide impetus for the study of the dynamics of choices between citizens, mayors, and firms. We use them to see what type of equilibrium can emerge. In particular, can an equilibrium exist between a bad governance (corrupt mayor) and good company (delivering services), and if yes is it unstable? Can we see a shift to good governance and well-performing companies as a result of a small perturbation (such as more political awareness from voters)? What are the chances that a citizen response using "voice" will emerge? Are solutions like the Bangalore Agenda Task Force,[7] where civil society interacts with the state to improve governance, replicable elsewhere? Can we explain the empirical finding for U.S. municipalities by Warner and Hefetz (2003) that municipalities relying more on private companies to deliver services also rank lower on voice and equity measures?

Our main reason for focusing on these examples in a globalized context is to reveal the rather seamy side to globalization, which co-exists with the benefits of globalization. The intensification of the exchanges and increased demands of citizens for good governance also comes with more sophisticated and "hidden" opportunities for bad governance. Typically, financial crimes and money laundering on an international scale make it more and more complex to dismantle embezzlement and corruption in countries that are already exposed to bad governance and lack of transparency. In other words, globalization could amplify good or bad governance. Cities and regions with good governance would thus tend to become even more efficient, while cities that are suffering from bad governance would become even worse, especially in most African cities and in the old industrial centers in Europe and Central Asia, where it is difficult for the citizens to "exit" from the grip of local authorities.

Conclusions and Further Research

In this chapter, we have used game theory to show that the dynamics of interaction among citizens, mayors, and firms, within a context of globalization, can improve the performance of cities. This framework attempts to derive the nature of causality from globalization to good governance and from local accountability to good governance. In fact, our analysis shows that both globalization and local accountability matter, but that the interaction between globalization and good governance should lead to better performance than local accountability by itself or globalization in the absence of local accountability. We have shown that, when firms try to influence city leaders and go unchecked, city performance is likely to suffer.

What firms and citizens know also matters for good governance. Thus, making a range of critical information publicly available, for example, on a city website, improves the possibility of good governance and can lead to better quality of life for the city's citizens. Better information provides better means to control public accountability. In this chapter, we have focused on information access through websites and have not looked at media's role as a watchdog, which has been well studied by others (see Sassen 2002 for an extensive review). What comes out of our work is that cities can do a lot using technology to improve the access to information.

Our results also indicate that history matters. A methodology that captures the dynamics over time can shed light on some of the difficult issues surrounding urban governance. Such analysis would be relevant to understand the high urbanization rates in Africa, which have come with little increased welfare for cities, limited economic growth for countries, scarce foreign direct investment for firms, and well-known challenges for governance. Chapter 4 explores these challenges further. Additional research on African cities, using a historical methodology, could also shed light on this difficult topic.

Annex 5.1. Proof of the Nash Equilibrium Outcome

Theorem: Fudenberg and Tirole (1991). The terminal state of such a game, where citizens, mayors, and firms choose from the set of actions shown above is Nash Equilibrium.

Proof: Fix a Nash Equilibrium at α^*, which is a building block of a repeated game where the citizen, mayor, and firm are playing over a fixed time period T (mayoral electoral cycle over five years). All three players must play (loyal, satisfy, locate) at this stage, since doing so increases their period-T payoff and since there are no future periods in which they will be punished, by earning less than their reservation utility. This is true for any period history h^T that has positive probability under a^*.

The static equilibrium for each player is $a^*(i)$ with the terminal reward phase being $g_i(\alpha^*(i)) > v_i$. At this stage, players receive strictly more than their reservation utility (min-max value) v_i.

For a repeated cycle $\bar{R}$ (with R large enough) each player prefers payoff v_i followed by the R-cycle terminal phase of (loyal, satisfy, locate), to getting the largest possible payoff $\max_a g_i(a)$ in one period and then being min-maxed for $R.I$ periods (Fudenberg and Tirole 1991).

Select a small ε such that $v + \varepsilon$; $\varepsilon > 0$ and $\{a(t)\}$ is a deterministic cycle of length $T - R.I$ whose average payoffs are within ε of payoff v. Each player plays according to the deterministic cycle (loyal, satisfy, locate). If any player deviates from this path when there are more than $R.I$ periods left, then min-max that player for the remainder of the game. If player agrees with $\{a(t)\}$ until there are $R.I$ periods left, then follow the R-cycle terminal phase for the remainder of the game.

Notes

1. Today there are 36,565 municipalities in metropolitan France, among which around 32,000 comprise less than 2,000 inhabitants (see Annex 5.2). In comparison, there are 14,727 municipalities in Germany; 8,070 in Italy; 8,027 in Spain; and 522 in the United Kingdom.

2. Measuring city population is difficult because there a few common definitions across countries. The convention we use in this chapter is based on measured urban population from latest census within a known municipal administration. This definition was developed by City Mayors in a conference in July 2003 and more details can be found on-line at "World Cities, 2003". http://www.citymayors.com.

3. A popular application of game theory, which has results similar to our work, can be found on a website (Civilization Fanatics Center 2005) that has messages from players using mathematical games. There is a game on the internet that allows players to start off from scratch and build cities, adding infrastructure, different forms of government, and degrees of corruption and waste in managing natural resources, as well as production (http://forum.civfanatics.com, accessed on August 24, 2005). In this website, a number of players exchange strategies for the game. One player, known as "Alexman" who presents his results under a title "Do you think you understand corruption?" shows after many plays, that there is a limit to corruption at about 95 percent of cities, meaning that there is always room for corruption to be fought and thus it does not exist in a stable equilibrium. The specification we have, where the citizens can put pressure for good governance, is such a control. We represent this pressure as a small variable, which varies according to the choices made by the citizen, whether to be loyal and do nothing, exercise voice or leave the city.

4. We assume that, for the mayor, refusing influence by firms in the short run is better than ignoring citizens, since citizens may applaud the mayor for not being influenced by firms (unless the citizens do not know about the firm's influence).

5. The Kearney index is for country-level globalization measures, whereas the Taylor Index is for specific cities. See Chapter 3 and Kaufmann, Léautier, and Mastruzzi (2004) for more detail on these indexes.

6. An analysis done by Kaufmann and Mastruzzi (2004) and available by request to the authors indicates that when you use a broader set of cities, including developing country cities, there is a positive relationship between globalization and quality of life, even though variation remains.

7. The Bangalore Agenda Task Force is a Bangalore-based citizens' monitoring initiative that generates report cards on public services using systematic citywide feedback from citizens. See Paul 2002.

References

Benoit, J. P., and V. Krishna. 1985. "Finitely Repeated Games." *Econometrica* 53: 890–904.

Besson, Danielle. 2002. "L'investissement des administrations publiques locales – Influence de la décentralisation et du cycle des élections municipales." *INSEE Première* (October).

Chandernagor, André. 1993. *Les maires en France – XIXème-XXème siècles.* Paris: Fayard.

Chandler, Tertius. 1987. *Four Thousand Years of Urban Growth: An Historical Census.* Lewiston: St. Gourds.

Chase-Dunn, Christopher, and Alice Willard. 1993. "Systems of Cities and World Systems: Settlement Size Hierarchies and Cycles of Political Centralization 2000 BC to 1988 AD." Annual Convention of the International Studies Association. Acapulco.

City Mayors. 2003. "World Cities." On-line at http://www.citymayors.com/features/urban_areas1.html.

Civilization Fanatics Center. 2005. "Do you think you understand corruption?" On-line at http://forum.civfanatics.com.

Cour des Comptes. 1997. "La gestion des services publics locaux d'eau et d'assainissement." Paris.

De Long, B. J., and A. Shleifer. 1992. *Princes and Merchants: European City Growth before the Industrial Revolution.* Cambridge, MA: National Bureau of Economic Research and Harvard University (issued in March; revised in December).

Durkheim, Emile. 1903. "Les communes françaises du Moyen-Age." *L'Année sociologique* 6.

Duval, Guillaume. 1996. "Etat des lieux." *Alternatives Economiques* (April).

Escobar, Jésus, and Dennis Hodgson. 1998. "Honors Seminar: The City in American Imagination." Syllabus, Fairfield University, Fairfield, CN. On-line at http://www.faculty.fairfield.edu/faculty/hodgson/Courses/city/origins/.

Estache, Antonio, and Eugene Kouassi. 2002. "Sector organization, governance, and the inefficiency of African water utilities." Policy Research Working Paper. Washington, DC: World Bank.

Foreign Policy. 2002. A.T. Kearney/Foreign Policy Magazine Globalization Index 2002. On-line at http://www.foreignpolicy.com/wwwboard/g-index2.php. Released as "Globalization's Last Hurrah." *Foreign Policy* (Jan/Feb): 38–51.

Francillon, Claude. 1996. "Grenoble conclut un nouveau contrat d'eau avec la Lyonnaise." *Le Monde* (March 24).

Fudenberg, D., and J. Tirole. 1991. *Game Theory.* Cambridge, MA: MIT Press.

Georges, Jocelyne. 1990. *Histoire des maires 1789–1939*. Paris: Editions Christian de Bartillat.

Gibbons, R. 1992. *Game Theory for Applied Economists*. Princeton, NJ: Princeton University Press.

Hamblin, Jane Dora. 1977. The First Cities. New York: Time-Life.

Henderson, V. J., and A. J. Venables. 2004. *The Dynamics of City Formation: Finance and Governance*. Discussion Paper 4638. London: Centre for Economic Policy Research.

Hirschmann, A. O. 1970. *Exit, Voice, and Loyalty: Responses to the Decline in Firms, Organizations, and States*. Cambridge, MA: President and Fellows of Harvard College. (January).

Huot, Jean-Louis, Jean-Paul Thalman, and Dominique Valbelle. 1990. *Naissances des Cités*. Paris: Nathan.

Inciyan, Erich. 1996. "La Générale des eaux reconnaît des financements politiques illégaux." *Le Monde* (October 26).

INSEE (Institut National de la Statistique et des etudes economiques).1999. On-line at http://en.wikipedia.org/wiki/Commune_in_France.

Kaufmann, Daniel, and Aart Kraay. 2002. "Growth without Governance." World Bank Policy Research Working Paper 2928. Washington DC: World Bank.

Kaufmann, Daniel, Frannie Léautier, and Massimo Mastruzzi. 2004. "An Empirical Exploration into Global Determinants of Urban Performance." World Bank Institute Working Papers and Articles (Discussion Paper). Washington, DC: World Bank. On-line at http:/www.worldbank.org/wbi/governance/pdf/govcity.pdf.

Lambarde, William. 1570. "Stack of Statutes." In *A Perambulation of Kent*. Archived Books.

Léautier, Frannie, and A. Lemer. 2003. "Perspectives on Globalization of Infrastructure." World Bank Institute Working Papers. Washington, DC: World Bank.

Le Wino, Frédéric. 1994. "Le scandale du prix de l'eau." *Le Point* (April 30).

Mercer Human Resource Consulting. 2004. "Quality of Life Index." On-line athttp://www.mercerHR.com. Accessed in August 2005.

Paul, André. 2000. *Les Manuscrits de la Mer Morte*. Paris: Bayard Editions/Centurion.

Paul, S. 2002. *Holding the State to Account*. Bangalore: Books for Change.

Pujas, Véronique. 2000. "Corruption via party financing in France." Paper presented at a workshop on corruption and political party funding in La Pietra, Italy, October.

Rausch, James. 1995. "Bureaucracy, Infrastructure and Economic Growth: Evidence from U.S. Cities During the Progressive Era." *American Economic Review* 85 (September 1995): 968–79.

Royal Borough of Kingston upon Thames. 2005. "History of the Office of Mayor." Based on *Civic Ceremonial; A Handbook, History and Guide for Mayors, Councillors and Officers*, 4th ed., by Paul Milward. On-line at http://www.kingston.gov.uk/council_and_democracy/.../history_of_the_office_of_mayor.ht.

Sassen, S. 2002. "Global Cities and Diasporic Networks: Microsites in Global Civil Society." Chapter 9 in *Global Civil Society 2002*. London: Centre for the Study of Global Governance.

Taylor, P. J., and D. R. F. Walker. 2001. "World City Network: Data Matrix Construction and Analysis." From the GaWC Research Group and Network, Data Set 6. Based on primary data collected by J. V. Beaverstock, R. G. Smith, and P. J. Taylor for the ESRC project "The Geographical Scope of London as a World City." London: Economic and Social Research Council. On-line at http://www.lboro.ac.uk/gawc/.

United Nations CyberSchoolbus. 1996. "A Brief History of Urban Expansion." On-line at http://www.un.org/cyberschoolbus/habitat/units/un02pg01.asp.

Warner, M., and A. Hefetz. 2003. "Contracting: Theoretical Propositions, Empirical Realities." Paper presented to the Economic Policy Institute, Washington DC, April 4.

World Economic Forum. 2003. Executive Opinion Survey (EOS). Geneva.

6

Explaining Urban Performance: Globalization, Technology, and Scale

Daniel Kaufmann, Frannie Léautier, and Massimo Mastruzzi

Even a casual look at a city while visiting as a tourist or on a business trip indicates the quality of life that residents of the city enjoy or suffer. The casual observer is not aware of the quality of governance of the city, but sees the outcome of such governance. It turns out that this is a conundrum that has challenged visitors and investors historically. De Long and Shleifer (1992) look at the evolution of European cities over a number of centuries from a governance perspective, using the size of the city as an indicator of performance. They investigate whether the city was governed by a prince (monarchy) or merchants (constitutional committee or business interests) and what effect the quality of governance has had on city size.

In Chapter 3 and elsewhere, we have tried to dig deeper into the question of the determinants of good city governance (see also Kaufmann, Léautier, and Mastruzzi 2004). We focused on whether there is an interaction between governance and globalization and, if so, how that interaction affects the observed performance of a city. We observed a differential impact of governance and globalization on a city's ability to deliver infrastructure services, and were curious about what was driving this result.

In this chapter, we consider a number of factors that may account for the observed differences in city performance. We investigate the long-run trends of city performance, using city size as a measure of performance, building on a concept initially used by De Long and Shleifer (1992). We then seek to confirm that the long-run trends are supported by more diverse data on performance by comparing city profiles on access to basic services (water, sewerage, and electricity). This chapter provides further empirical investigation of the theoretical model we introduced in Chapter 5 and seeks to expand some of the findings that were particularly interesting, such as the role of the citizen in driving change at the city level toward good governance.

We look at the particular case of access to information, both by citizens and by firms, and use a proxy of access to communication services, such as telephone lines, cellular phones, and the internet. We focus on these types of services because of the impact such services have on the ability of citizens to participate in decision making and get access to information. Finally, we look further at quality of life across a number of cities, on the assumption that a casual observer would observe quality-of-life differentials across cities.[1]

Using these data, we test the conjecture that the choices citizens and firms have over what services to demand and use from a municipal government do have an impact on whether and how they will pressure their governments to perform. Technology is offering opportunities to citizens and firms, allowing them to function and cope even in poor governance settings, while at the same time also offering citizens easier opportunities to exercise *voice*. It is relatively easier to send an e-mail than to make a phone call, which requires a person at the other end of the line, or even to travel to a municipal office and physically lodge a complaint. We surmise, however, that the presence of some technologies for *choice* would weaken citizen pressure for accountability, which would tend to reduce the quality of city governance and the overall quality of life in the city. Similarly, in the presence of such technologies, firms seeking to locate in the city would be less bothered by poor city governance, because the firms could always provide their own services. Such firms would have less incentive to pressure the local governments for improved performance. A citizen who can provide her own water service through a private well would have less reason to use *voice*, and a firm that can have its own electricity service through a private generator would have little need to *influence* the municipality to improve performance.

Our main argument is that technology offers citizens and firms choices to exit networked systems and self-provide such services as telephones—by using mobile phones instead of line-systems or having a private well instead of relying on piped municipal water. We conjecture that the presence of technological choices, which allow citizens and firms to exit from a poorly performing utility or municipal service, renders less relevant the effects of both globalization and good governance on city performance. If this conjecture holds, then cities will have high performance with respect to such services even if they are poorly governed or less connected to the pressures of globalization. In the following sections, we explicitly test this hypothesis.

Data

We use data from several sources to test the hypotheses outlined above. Data taken from Chandler (1987) allows us to look at the long-run trends in city population, checking whether the hypothesis that cities wane and grow has held over time and, if there is a good basis to expect this pattern, to examine the role that citizens and firms play in that process. We extract data for 60 cities from this database, which spans close to 5,000 years from 3100 BC to 1975, and we augment it with data from the City Mayors (2003) dataset to bring the trends up to the year 2005, thus covering a span of over 5,000 years of data. We refer to these data as the "Chandler" database.

A rich data set originally used by De Long and Shleifer (1992) includes the performance of 77 European cities from 1050 to 1800. The size of cities is used as the indicator of long-run performance, with the assumption that, if a city is well governed, it should attract new residents and keep those already present. De Long and Shleifer construct these data from three original sources: (a) Russell (1972), which includes European cities before the year 1500; (b) de Vries (1984), which has populations in European cities between 1500 and 1800; and (c) Bairoch and others (1988), which has data on European city populations from the year 800 to 1850. We use the three data sets together and refer to them as the "Bairoch-Russell-de Vries" database.

For city performance data, we use data from UNCHS (1998) for access to services such as sewerage, water, electricity, and phone lines, and data from the World Economic Forum's Executive Opinion Survey (2003) for other service variables at the city level, such as access to cell phones, internet in schools, and quality of electricity and overall infrastructure services. The full sample of data from this set, which we refer to in Chapter 3 as the Kaufmann-Léautier-Mastruzzi dataset, consists of data for 412 cities.

For city population, country urbanization, and country income, we use data from the *World Development Indicators* (World Bank 2001 and 2002). We complement the data on city performance with measures of quality of life obtained from Mercer Human Resource Consulting (2002). The Mercer dataset contains data on 215 cities and provides an evaluation of quality of life in these cities based on detailed assessment and evaluations of 39 key quality-of-life determinants, grouped under political and social environment, economic environment, sociocultural environment, medical and health considerations, schools and education, public services and transportation, recreation, consumer goods, housing, and natural environment. As such, it is a good complement to the UNCHS and EOS datasets.

Patterns from History

When looking at long-run trends in the size of cities, it is striking to see that there are three distinct phenomena (Table 6.1). First, very few cities are capable of maintaining top performance, when performance is measured in terms of the size of the recorded population, following a convention developed by De Long and Shleifer (1992). We have referred to this phenomenon as "staying power" in Chapter 3.

Second, the absolute size of the largest city seems to grow and then diminish. See, for example the pattern of growth between 3100 BC (when Memphis, Egypt, was the largest city with a population over 30,000 and maintained this status for nearly 1,000 years) and 25 BC, when Rome was the largest with a population of 450,000. The population of the largest city then diminished between 25 BC and 637, only to grow again to over 1 million in 775, with Baghdad taking the largest city position. The pattern between 1825 and 2005 shows similar reversals.

Third, the presence of European cities is seen around 25 BC, with Rome assuming the position of largest city. In the year 100, Rome was still the largest city in the world, and European cities represented about 10 percent of the ten largest cities. By 1000 Rome had been replaced by Cordova, Spain, but Europe still had only 10 percent of its cities in the top ten largest cities. In 1500, Paris replaced Cordoba, but Europe still

Table 6.1. *City with Largest Recorded Population in the Past 5,000 Years*

Year	Population	City	Country
3100 BC	30,000	Memphis	Egypt
2030 BC	65,000	Ur	Iraq
612 BC	200,000	Babylon	Iraq
195 BC	400,000	Changan	China
25 BC	450,000	Rome	Italy
340	400,000	Constantinople	Turkey
637	400,000	Changan	China
775	1,000,000	Baghdad	Iraq
935	450,000	Cordova	Spain
1825	900,000	London	United Kingdom
1925	1,100,000	New York	United States
1965	23,000,000	Tokyo	Japan
2005	10,000,000	Seoul	Korea

Source: Data constructed from Chandler 1987.

Figure 6.1. *Largest City Population over Time*

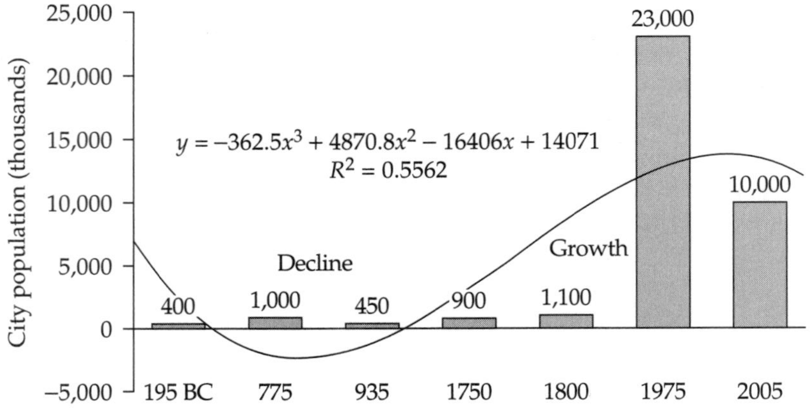

$$y = -362.5x^3 + 4870.8x^2 - 16406x + 14071$$
$$R^2 = 0.5562$$

Source: Population data taken from Chandler 1987.

had only 10 percent of its cities in the top most populous cities in the world. It is in 1800 that Europe has 30 percent of its cities in the top ten, with London replacing Paris as largest of all. By 1900, Europe had 60 percent of the cities in the top ten, with London still the largest—the first city to have a population above 5 million. By 1950, Europe's share of the largest cities had dropped to 40 percent, with London having been replaced by New York—the first city to have a population above 10 million.

Figure 6.1 shows these trends in more detail. Because of the pattern of growth and waning in the absolute size of cities and also of the presence of Europe in the last 5,000 years, we take a special look at the pattern of growth of European cities in the next section. We compare the performance of European cities using the "Bairoch-Russell-de Vries" dataset in Table 6.2, where the number of residents in those cities is recorded against different time periods.

From the long-run trends, it is evident that cities such as London or Paris were mere villages in 1050, each with a population of about 10,000 people. These cities grew to almost a million and a half million people, respectively, in 1800, and have populations of more than 7 million and 10 million, respectively, in their metropolitan areas today. Contrast this pattern with cities such as Palermo and Cordova, which had 350,000 and 450,000 people, respectively, in 1050. Palermo shrunk to 140,000 people in 1800, while Cordova had no population recorded by the year 1500. Cross-comparing the situation of Cordova in the "Bairoch-Russell-de Vries" dataset with the "Chandler" dataset, we see that Cordova was recorded as the largest known city in 935.[2]

An analysis of the historical growth of cities reveals three main patterns: expansion, decline, and bouncing back (Table 6.3), confirming the pattern from the "Chandler" dataset in Figure 6.1 and Table 6.1. Cities such as London, Paris, and Amsterdam started off as small villages and continued to grow. They are still large and important cities today. Other cities, such as Cordova, Salerno, and Cartagena, declined from a significant heyday. Some cities, such as Venice, Seville, and Florence, fluctuated with rising and falling fortunes, but bounced back. Cities remained in a period of long decline like Granada, or bounced back like Bordeaux and Prague. Some cities, such as Pavia and Musina, were stable and maintained almost a constant population over long periods of time.

Table 6.2. *Population of Major Cities, 1050–1800*
(thousands of residents)

City	1050	1200	1330	1500	1650	1800
London	10	25	35	50	350	948
Paris	10	110	150	225	400	550
Naples	30	30	125	125	300	430
Vienna					70	247
Amsterdam					120	217
Dublin						200
Lisbon	15		35	65	150	195
Berlin						172
Madrid					100	168
Rome	35	35	30	55	110	153
Palermo	350	150	51	55	100	140
Venice	45	70	110	100	140	138
Milan		100	100	100	120	135
Hamburg					40	130
Lyon				50	60	109
Copenhagen					65	101
Marseille			31	45	70	101
Barcelona			48			100
Seville	90	80	90	45	80	96
Bordeaux				50		96
Genoa		30	100	58	64	90
Manchester						84
Edingburgh						83
Turin						82
Florence	15	60	95	55	74	81
Valencia		26	44	42	50	80
Rouen			35	40	60	80
Nantes						77
Stockholm						76
Prague				70	50	76
Cordova	450	60	60			
Salerno	50	30				
Regensberg	40					
Toledo	37	35	42			
Barbastro	35					
Cartagena	33					
Mainz	30					
Merida	30					
Almeria	27					
Granada	26	60	150	70	70	70
Speyer	25					
Palma	25	30				
Laon	25	40				
Elvira	22					
Cologne	21	50	54	45	40	
Trier	20					
Caen	20					

(table continues on following page)

Table 6.2. (Continued)

City	1050	1200	1330	1500	1650	1800
Tours	20			60		
Verona	20	33		50	40	40
Worms	20					
Ypres		40				
Bologna		35	40	50	63	
Narbonne		31				
Pavia		30				
Messina		30				
Angers		30	33			
Ferrara		27	36	42		
Orleans		27		50		
Metz		27				
Cremona		25	40	40	40	40
Siena			50			
Bruges			40	35		
Malaga			40	42		
Aquila			40			
Pisa			38			
Montpellier			35			
St.-Omer			35			
Toulouse			30			
Ghent				55	40	
Brescia				49	40	40
Nuremberg				38	40	
Antwerp					60	
Brussels					60	
Danzig					60	
Leiden					55	
Caen	20					
Leon		40				
Number of cities reporting	30	30	31	30	33	34

Note: Because of the methods used to collect data for medieval cities, a blank does not necessarily mean that there was no one living there, but that there was no record of people living there, which is an indicator that the importance of the city had diminished.

Source: Taken from the "Bairoch-Russell-de Vries" dataset originally used by De Long and Shleifer (1992).

The long-run patterns, which follow the general shape of the polynomial in Figure 6.1 using the "Chandler" data set, indicate that, once started, cities tend to remain and grow (37 out of 77,which is nearly 50 percent). However, a good share of cities can decline and never recover (19 out of 77, or close to 25 percent). Those that can bounce back from decline exhibit a (∪-shaped or saw-toothed curve or remain stable over time. These represent the remaining 25 percent of cities, of which only 7 (10 percent) truly have a long history of bouncing back. We would like to particularly explore the cities that were able to bounce back to see what factors led them to do so. In particular, what distinguishes cities such as Palermo, Venice, Bordeaux, Genoa, Seville, Florence, and Prague from those that declined?

Table 6.3. *Average Population Growth of Major Cities, 1050–1800*
(percent change over the entire period)

City	Expansion	Bounce back	Decline
London	98		
Paris	96		
Naples	93		
Vienna	100		
Amsterdam	93		
Dublin	100		
Lisbon	92		
Berlin	100		
Madrid	100		
Rome	77		
Palermo		−150	
Venice		67	
Milan	89		
Hamburg	100		
Lyon	82		
Copenhagen	85		
Marseille	85		
Barcelona	85		
Seville		6	
Bordeaux		84	
Genoa		83	
Manchester	100		
Edingburgh	100		
Turin	100		
Florence		81	
Valencia	81		
Rouen	81		
Nantes	100		
Stockholm	100		
Prague		80	
Cordova			−650
Salerno			−67
Regensberg			−60
Toledo	12		
Barbastro			−40
Cartagena			−32
Mainz			−20
Merida			−20
Almeria			−8
Granada		63	
Speyer		0	
Palma		17	
Laon		17	
Elvira		12	
Cologne		53	
Trier		20	
Caen		20	

(table continues on following page)

Table 6.3. *(Continued)*

City	Expansion	Bounce back	Decline
Tours	67		
Verona		60	
Worms		0	
Ypres			−33
Bologna	44		
Narbonne			−3
Pavia		0	
Messina		0	
Angers	14		
Ferrara		33	
Orleans	46		
Metz	10		
Cremona		38	
Siena			−43
Bruges			−14
Malaga	5		
Aquila			−14
Pisa			−9
Montpellier			0
St.-Omer			0
Toulouse	14		
Ghent			−8
Brescia			−23
Nuremberg	5		
Antwerp	20		
Brussels	20		
Danzig	20		
Leiden	27		
Caen	20		
Leon			−33
Number of cities reporting	37	21	19

Source: Constructed from the "Bairoch-Russell-de Vries" dataset originally used by De Long and Shleifer (1992).

The Effect of City Size

De Long and Shleifer (1992) linked good governance to city size, showing that well-governed cities grew and poorly governed cities declined. Using data we constructed from various sources, we ask a series of questions on the performance of cities. In particular, we seek to verify whether cities that have declined over time have issues with governance, as De Long and Shleifer (1992) claim? Can we find the same patterns of city size and growth in modern times? Can we link corruption in access to utilities and in taxes to city performance as measured by city size? What are the effects of the size and characteristics of the city? Based on the data in Tables 6.4 to 6.7, we draw the following preliminary conclusions.

Does Size Matter?

The size of the city population does seem to have an impact on some services (Tables 6.4 through 6.6). For example, in more populous cities, it seems more difficult to get good access to services, such as sewerage, water, electricity, and telephones. The OECD countries seem to perform better in this regard, indicating that with increasing wealth the constraint of city population disappears (see also the positive effect of income on city performance). However, there appears to be no adverse "megacity" effect—cities with populations of more than 5 million do not perform below others in a range of access and quality variables (see Table 6.8). While diseconomies of scale may exist in particular determinants of performance for megacities (complexity of management, for instance), they may be neutralized by agglomeration (scale) economies in other dimensions (for example, lumpy investments). From Table 6.4 we do not see any evidence that large cities are better or worse managed than smaller cities. If not size, then what matters?

For cities that are not mega-size, there appears to be some evidence of a simple, nonlinear effect of city size (compare Table 6.5 and 6.6 and the population columns in Table 6.8. In Table 6.5, which displays results for the non-OECD sample, we see that, for all measures of city performance, whether access to sewerage, water, electricity, and phone lines, or even when looking at the quality of infrastructure and electricity services, small cities (those with "low" rating in city population) outperform large cities (those with "high" rating in city population). This effect, seems to diminish when looking at cities in OECD countries, as shown in Table 6.6, where this result holds only with respect to access to sewerage and phone lines, with very

Table 6.4. *City Performance by City Size and Country Development in the Full Sample*

| | City population 2002 | | Development measures | | | |
| | | | Country urbanization 2002 | | Country income per capita, 2001 | |
Variable	Low	High	Low	High	Low	High
Access to sewerage (%, UN)	86	69	59	93	60	97
Access to water (%, UN)	90	79	71	98	72	100
Access to electricity (%, UN)	91	89	86	97	84	100
Access to telephone lines 1 (%, UN)	64	50	43	85	38	93
Access to telephone lines 2 (1–7, EOS)	5.3	5.3	4.7	6.2	4.6	6.2
Access to cellular phones (1–7, EOS)	6.0	6.0	5.7	6.5	5.6	6.5
Access to internet in schools (1–7, EOS)	3.9	3.7	3.2	4.7	3.0	4.9
Quality of infrastructure (1–7, EOS)	3.7	4.0	3.1	4.8	3.0	4.9
Quality of electricity (1–7, EOS)	4.6	4.6	4.0	5.5	3.8	5.8
Overall number of cities	205	205	183	183	212	200

Note: The full sample comprises 412 cities. Each column variable was segmented into two equal samples, below and above the median value of full sample.

Source: Data labeled as UN is taken from UNCHS 1998. Data labeled as EOS is taken from the World Economic Forum 2003. City population and country urbanization data are taken from the *World Development Indicators* (World Bank 2002). Income per capita data come from Summers and Heston 1984. Other income and population data are from the *CIA World Factbook*. (CIA 2005).

Table 6.5. *City Performance by City Size and Country Development in the Non-OECD Sample*

| | City population 2002 | | Development measures | | | |
| | | | Country urbanization 2002 | | Country income per capita, 2001 | |
Variable	Low	High	Low	High	Low	High
Access to sewerage (%, UN)	80	61	56	76	53	83
Access to water (%, UN)	90	73	66	89	66	93
Access to electricity (%, UN)	91	86	82	94	82	95
Access to telephone lines 1 (%, UN)	65	45	36	69	31	74
Access to telephone lines 2 (1–7, EOS)	5.1	4.6	4.5	5.3	4.3	5.4
Access to cellular phones (1–7, EOS)	5.8	5.7	5.6	6.0	5.4	6.1
Access to internet in schools (1–7, EOS)	3.7	2.9	3.0	3.8	2.6	4.0
Quality of infrastructure (1–7, EOS)	3.3	3.2	3.0	3.6	2.8	3.7
Quality of electricity (1–7, EOS)	4.3	3.8	3.7	4.5	3.4	4.7
Overall number of cities	136	136	124	107	137	137

Note: The non-OECD sample comprises 274 cities. Each column variable was segmented into two equal samples, below and above the median value of full sample.

Source: Data labeled as UN is taken from UNCHS 1998. Data labeled as EOS is taken from the World Economic Forum 2003. City population and country urbanization data are taken from the *World Development Indicators* (World Bank 2002). Income per capita data come from Summers and Heston 1984. Other income and population data are from the *CIA World Factbook.* (CIA 2005).

small differences in performance across "low" and "high" population cities, and the reverse pattern for all other variables of city performance.

In Table 6.6, we see that this effect is more pronounced when cities are classified by size as small, mid-size, large, and mega. In particular, we observe a (∪-shaped size-performance curve: mid-size cities with population between half a million and a million perform worse than both their smaller and their larger counterparts. Relatively small *and* large cities, in fact, perform similarly. The same relationship emerges when using a quality-of-life index (see Table 6.7).

What Is the Role of Good Management?

It is almost as if mid-size cities suffer from management diseconomies compared with their smaller counterparts, without benefiting yet from the scale economies of larger cities. This may be due to the large, lumpy nature of infrastructure investments (which may be easier to manage in cities larger than 1 million). This holds even when using a different data set, as in Table 6.7. We compare quality of life taken from the Mercer Index (Mercer Human Resource Consulting 2002), segmented according to city population. The result confirms the (∪-shape pattern, indicating that small cities have better quality of life than medium and large cities, but that some large cities, and even some megacities, can provide a high quality of life. The panel data shows the existence of large cities that are well performing in terms of quality of life, as well as small cities that are well performing with high quality of life. Have the dynamics played out to weed out those that are not well governed? This requires a much closer look at mid-size cities.

Table 6.6. *City Performance by City Size and Country Development in the OECD Sample*

Variable	City population 2002		Development measures			
			Country urbanization 2002		Country income per capita, 2001	
	Low	High	Low	High	Low	High
Access to sewerage (%, UN)	100	99	99	100	99	100
Access to water (%, UN)	100	100	99	100	100	100
Access to electricity (%, UN)	100	100	100	100	100	100
Access to telephone lines 1 (%, UN)	94	95	92	100	84	96
Access to telephone lines 2 (1–7, EOS)	6.4	6.5	6.1	6.8	6.4	6.5
Access to cellular phones (1–7, EOS)	6.6	6.7	6.5	6.8	6.6	6.7
Access to internet in schools (1–7, EOS)	5.3	5.3	4.7	5.8	5.0	5.8
Quality of infrastructure (1–7, EOS)	5.4	5.5	4.9	6.0	5.2	5.8
Quality of electricity (1–7, EOS)	6.3	6.1	5.8	6.6	6.0	6.4
Overall number of cities	69	69	72	63	72	66

Note: The OECD sample comprises 138 cities. Each column variable was segmented into two equal samples, below and above the median value of full sample.

Source: Data labeled as UN is taken from UNCHS 1998. Data labeled as EOS is taken from the World Economic Forum 2003. City population and country urbanization data are taken from the *World Development Indicators* (World Bank 2002). Income per capita data come from Summers and Heston 1984. Other income and population data are from the *CIA World Factbook.* (CIA 2005).

Table 6.7. *City Size and Quality of Life in the Non-OECD Sample*

Variable	Small cities <0.5 million	Midsize cities 0.5<p<1million	Large cities 1<p<5million	Megacities >5million
Quality of life (0–100)	69.0	65.5	61.5	64.7
Overall number of cities	13	20	53	19

Source: Mercer Human Resource Consulting 2002 and 2005.

Is It Cities or Urban Agglomerations That Count?

Cities tend to be better governed than nonurban agglomerations, such as large villages and small towns, as the country urbanization indicator (a measure of the share of a country's population living in cities) shows overall better results when it is high than when it is low, even for more advanced economies (Table 6.4 through 6.6). So, there is something distinctive about cities that can produce good governance; it is not just about agglomerating large numbers of people in one place. Organization and management seem to matter, and that is why large cities can be as well governed as small cities.

The Effect of Technology and Service Characteristics

Contrast the access to business telephone lines, personal telephones, and cell phones in Tables 6.8 and 6.9.[3] The role of governance and globalization is almost

Table 6.8. *City Performance by City Attributes in the Non-OECD Sample*

					Population			
	Port city		Capital city		Small <0.5 million	Midsize 0.5<p<1 million	Large 1<p<5 million	Mega >5 million
Variable	No	Yes	No	Yes				
Access to sewerage (%, UN)	50	41	42	49	80	59	56	81
Access to water (%, UN)	64	62	59	65	90	69	71	84
Access to electricity (%, UN)	79	70	73	76	91	77	90	83
Access to telephone lines 1 (%, UN)	90	81	84	87	65	40	44	54
Access to telephone lines 2 (1–7, EOS)	4.8	5.1	5.0	4.7	5.1	4.2	4.5	5.5
Access to cellular phones (1–7, EOS)	5.7	5.9	5.8	5.7	5.8	5.6	5.6	6.0
Access to internet in schools (1–7, EOS)	3.3	3.5	3.5	3.0	3.7	2.6	2.8	3.6
Quality of infrastructure (1-7, EOS)	3.2	3.4	3.3	3.3	3.3	2.7	3.3	3.4
Quality of electricity (1-7, EOS)	4.2	4.0	4.1	4.0	4.3	3.6	3.8	4.1
Overall number of cities	167	106	178	96	135	29	86	22

Note: The non-OECD sample comprises 274 cities.

Source: Data labeled as UN is taken from UNCHS 1998. Data labeled as EOS is taken from the World Economic Forum 2003. City population and country urbanization data are taken from the *World Development Indicators* (World Bank 2002). Income per capita data come from Summers and Heston 1984. Other income and population data are from the *CIA World Factbook.* (CIA 2005).

neutralized as people and firms are able to get access to telephones or cell phones independently of the city's utility company, but are highly dependent on globalization and its pressures and good governance when it comes to lumpy investments, such as access to telephone lines. This is evident through the wider gap between well-governed and poorly governed global cities for access to the telephone lines, compared to a narrower gap in the difference between well-governed and less well-governed global cities in the access to telephones and to cell phones.

We do know that having a telephone line is critical for internet services and hence to the aspect of globalization that allows firms to exchange ideas and information, as well as co-produce services across multiple cities. The results in Tables 6.8 and 6.9 demonstrate what many have argued as the negative impact of the digital divide. As wireless technology becomes more available, the impact of this constraint will diminish.

In particular, the results provide evidence that in poorly governed and less global cities, if individuals and private companies are not totally regulated, they are creative enough to manage and globalize themselves where technology so permits. By contrast, even when technological leaps have occurred, but government involvement is still needed, technology alone will not deliver the goods. Witness the generally poor performance of poorly governed cities (whether local or global) and local cities in providing internet access in schools. Good governance and globalization still deliver advantages when it comes to heavily networked services and

Table 6.9. *City Performance by City Technology in the Non-OECD Sample*

Variable	City has a website		Web has information on budget		Web information on how to start a business	
	No	Yes	No	Yes	No	Yes
Access to sewerage (%, UN)	44	54	46	70	45	72
Access to water (%, UN)	62	68	63	92	62	90
Access to electricity (%, UN)	75	76	75	91	74	93
Access to telephone lines 1 (%, UN)	84	93	86	99	86	95
Access to telephone lines 2 (1–7, EOS)	4.8	5.3	4.9	5.7	4.9	5.6
Access to cellular phones (1–7, EOS)	5.7	6.1	5.8	6.1	5.8	6.0
Access to internet in schools (1–7, EOS)	3.3	3.4	3.3	3.4	3.3	3.5
Quality of infrastructure (1–7, EOS)	3.3	3.4	3.3	3.5	3.3	3.5
Quality of electricity (1–7, EOS)	4.1	4.0	4.1	3.8	4.1	4.6
Overall number of cities	210	58	262	6	256	12

Note: The non-OECD sample comprises 274 cities.

Source: Data labeled as UN is taken from UNCHS 1998. Data labeled as EOS is taken from the World Economic Forum 2003. City population and country urbanization data are taken from the *World Development Indicators* (World Bank 2002). Income per capita data come from Summers and Heston 1984. Other income and population data are from the *CIA World Factbook.* (CIA 2005).

infrastructure. These results are even more pronounced for the full data set including OECD countries (results available upon request).

The main reason for the differential performance of cities with respect to services such as access to water and electricity may be the fact that citizens do have alternatives when these services are not well provided. A resident can "exit" from city-provided services by digging a well, using private water vendors, or installing a generator for electricity.

Firms, too, can install their own infrastructure services, and many do so (Lee and Anas 1996). The real impact of globalization is seen for those services where it is difficult to exit, such as telephone lines for data-dependent businesses (internet) and networked sewerage services, or where the quality of infrastructure has to be superior to attract residents and firms. This is where the data is sharp enough to demonstrate the differential contribution of globalization at the city level.

This result of globalization can also be seen when you contrast performance indicators on access to electricity with those on the quality of electricity services (blackouts, power surges, brownouts), as shown in Tables 6.8 and 6.9. The access to electricity seems not to be correlated with any variable of governance or globalization. However, the quality of electricity services shows strong differentiation between well-governed and poorly governed cities, and the results hold for both local and global cities. Most people who have access to an unreliable electric grid with frequent brownouts or blackouts, but can exit the system and have their own generators, would do so (see Lee and Anas 1996 for evidence of this behavior in the case of firms and wealthy citizens in Nigeria). Such a tendency would likely happen in more global cities, where the demand by global firms for reliable electricity services may be higher, but has also been observed in cities in developing countries (Lee and Anas 1996).

The real difference in performance shows up in the quality of electricity, since companies may have made their own investments in self-generation to deal with brownouts or blackouts, but cannot undertake a more sizable investment to guarantee a reliable service by themselves. They have to rely for quality on the city utility, even if they can get access from self-generation. It is also clear from these results that good governance plays an important role in delivering quality of services over a longer period of time—the staying power of cities in terms of performance. This result is also strong for the overall quality of infrastructure in Tables 6.8 and 6.9.

We can draw the following conclusions: The impact of globalization and good governance does affect city performance in the quality of services delivered, particularly for electricity, but also for telephone lines that permit access to the internet. We refer here and reinterpret results originally presented in Tables 3.5 and 3.6 and in the correlation matrix in Annex 3.1 in Chapter 3, which relate to the electricity regressions. These regressions do not perform at all (some have negative adjusted R^2), except in the case of the quality of electricity, a measure of the reliability of service. These results are reproduced in Table 6.10.

Contrast the performance of the regressions in Table 6.10 with the performance of the regressions on the other three service delivery variables of access to telephones, water, sewerage, as well as the indicator of reliability of services as measured by the quality of infrastructure variable. We believe that this is due to the ability of citizens to use choice rather than voice, when it comes to such services, and hence the weak relationship between governance variables, many of which are measures of voice, as transmitted by political decisions at the city level.

The Effect of City Type

Are port cities, which tend to be more open to the world as a result of the transport and logistics services they offer, better governed? We use variables measuring the quality of governance to investigate this hypothesis. In Table 6.8, we see that port cities perform better than other city types when comparing indicators such as informal money laundering, diversion of public funds, and illegal party financing, but have the same issues as other cities when it comes to bribery in taxes, cost of imports, and bribery to affect laws. These results are also corroborated by the findings presented earlier in Table 3.6 and Annex 3.1, which included the regression results against port city and capital city dummy variables. The fact that we find three positive and significant governance variables with respect to port cities and three negative and significant governance variables with respect to capital cities indicates that the differential openness of port cities to the global network does make a difference in their governance outcomes, lending further support of the results from the data set of the UN Centre for Human Settlement (UNCHS).

In Table 6.8 we also see that port cities do better than nonport cities for all services that are related to data and communications (access to telephone lines, access to cellular phones, and access to the internet). This result is expected as the logistic dependencies of port cities are well documented.

We find no evidence of the superior performance of capital cities with respect to offering better services to their citizens in the areas of communications services (telephones, cell phones, internet) or quality of infrastructure, but we do with respect to local services such as sewerage, water, and electricity. Capital cities seem to serve a more local function than port cities.

Table 6.10. *The Impact of Technology and Its Exit Opportunities on Pressure for Improved Governance*

Variables	Access to water	Access to sewerage	Access to cell phones	Access to electriticy	Quality of electricity
Bribery in utility	+/'	+/'	++/***	0/0	++++/***
Control of corruption	+/**	0/*	++/**	0/*	++++/***
Number of cities	63	59	194	61	194
Adjusted R^2	0.28	0.29	0.24	0.11	0.50

Note: The sample includes 412 cities in 134 countries. Values for magnitude (+, 0, -) and significance (*, 0, ') in each cell were obtained by averaging results of 21 different ordinary least squares specifications. In particular, for each independent variable, for calculating the magnitude of the coefficient rating (left-hand side), we computed the product of the average coefficient magnitude across all specifications times twice the standard deviation of the variable. Then we assigned magnitude values according to the following criteria: for positive coefficients, we applied a "++++" for any value above 1.2, "+++" for any value between 0.7 and 1.2, "++" for any value between 0.4 and 0.7, "+" for any value between 0.1 and 0.4, and finally a "0" for any value below 0.1. Similarly, minus signs were applied to negative coefficients. For the rating on the significance of the coefficient in each cell (right hand side), we averaged the various significance levels across the 21 specifications, where *** indicates significance at 1 percent, ** indicates significance at 5 percent, * indicates significance at 10 percent and ' indicates significance at 15 percent. Values for number of cities and R2 were computed as simple averages across all specifications.

Source: All dependent variables drawn from UNCHS 1998 and World Bank 2003; control of corruption drawn from Kaufmann and Kraay 2002; and bribery in utility drawn from World Bank 2003.

The results in Table 6.9, where we specifically look at whether a city has a web portal or not and whether it posts information on the city budget or how to start a business in the city, are even more conclusive. All three indicators of good governance show a marked difference in performance with respect to access to services.

In particular, having a website and posting information on the budget in the website (a measure of voice and transparency for all types of citizens even those who are not geographically resident in a city) is correlated to superior access to services (Table 6.8). This is also true with respect to whether the website has information on how to start a business.

We caution that these results are derived from uncontrolled statistical averages for different population range segments, without controlling for other factors. Some of these effects may disappear once more controls are included, but that result would in part be due to some of the potential explanation of such nonlinear effects in the first place. Such work can be the subject of further research.

Implications for Research and Policy

In this chapter we attempted to contribute to the field of urban governance through an empirically based exploration of some key determinants of the performance of cities. We find evidence that port cities seem to be in general more dependent on good governance for the city performance variables that matter for globalization (access to cell phone, internet access) and that capital cities tend more to serve local service access better (water, sewerage, and electricity). In particular, we find out that there is (∪-shaped relationship between city size and city performance, with both small and large cities performing better than mid-size cities. This relationship, described in Table 6.8 based on data from the mid-1990s, remains strong when using more recent data, as was done in Chapter 3 (Tables 3.6 and Annex 3.1).

Future Research

There are a number of issues to consider for future research. The most pertinent of them is to explore the characteristics of services to citizens and their implications for choice, particularly when citizens can only partially exit, as in having a back up generator for electricity but still relying on the public grid for the bulk of the services, or when citizens can exit but choose to use voice. This is mainly because of the differential performance of the "reliability" indicator of service (as represented by the quality of electricity variable in Table 6.10) and the "access" indicator of service (as represented by the access to electricity variable in Table 6.10).

Future research can also look at the behavior of the firm and citizen together or separately. We have attempted in this chapter and in Chapters 3 and 5, to look at both the citizen and the firm, but we had to rely on different datasets for the analysis. A joint questionnaire that investigates situations where, say, firms exit but citizens do not, or vice versa, may shed light on not only the dynamics of technology, as we have done in this chapter, or voice, exit, and loyalty, as we have done in Chapter 5, but also the interface between the two.

Finally, while we were able to test many hypotheses using different sets of data, there is still a big data gap. Investing in collecting data at the city level, that can complement the rich historical data that exists could add a lot of potential to further verify these preliminary results.

Policy Considerations

We show that citizens and firms generally benefit when their city provides an interface with technology, especially through the World Wide Web. Technology can be leveraged to go further, particularly where there are obstacles to governance and globalization reforms at the city level. As we noted, some new technologies may offer a partial substitute for a lack of political will to implement reforms by the (city and country) public leadership. New technologies, such as mobile phones and internet computing, enable private firms and city residents to effectively become more globalized, thus overcoming some of the impact of poor governance and lack of leadership that may limit their city's performance. However, such a mitigating effect of technology can only be partial where governance and accountability is wanting, given the high mobility of residents, firms, and capital—they all have an "exit" option.

Furthermore, even as technological improvements will continue to provide individualized private solutions as substitutes for large-scale infrastructure provision, there always will be some services (given their economies of scale and indivisibility) for which the public sector will play an important role. For appropriate public and private-sector strategies, it becomes increasingly important for donor agencies and city managers alike to distinguish between different types of infrastructure services, depending on the technologies available and the particular characteristics of the city.

Notes

The authors benefited from the valuable assistance of Erin Hoffmann and Fatima Sheikh.

The margins of error in any governance, institutional quality, and urban dataset imply that interpretative caution is warranted in general, and in particular argue against inferring seemingly precise city or country rankings from the data. For details on data, visit: http://www.worldbank.org/wbi/governance/.

1. In Chapter 5 we used the Mercer Quality of Life Index for the year 2004 for the top 50 cities. In this chapter we look at a broader range of cities, but with older data, for the year 2002, since we also wanted to test the effects of a lag. Data for 2004 for all these cities were not obtained on time for the publication of this book, and hence we did not test for the same effects across two data time periods-a subject that we delegate to further research.

2. Because the city population data for the early years has been constructed from travelers' chronicles and other such data including census, when they existed, and because periods of war, such as those in Cordova during the eleventh, twelfth, and thirteenth centuries, prevented accurate establishment of data, it is difficult to state the actual population for cities such as Cordova. Thus, population for many cities has been left blank in Table 6.2.

3. We use two measures of access to telephones. One is the access of the general population to a phone line, which we refer to here as "access to telephones 1." The other measure is the access of businesses to telephones, which we refer to as "access to telephones 2." The main reason for the distinction is that businesses would have a telephone in the place of business, rather than a telephone line, which is offered to serve a general agglomeration of people. The first measure is what is commonly used as a measure of access, which is the ratio of number of telephone lines to the number of people, hence lines per person. The second measures is the number of telephones per business unit, to capture businesses that have more than one phone installed in their places of business.

References

Bairoch, Paul, Jean Batou, and Pierre Chèvre. 1988. *La Population des Villes Européenes de 800 á 1850*. Geneva : Librairie Droz.

Chandler, Tertius. 1987. *Four Thousand Years of Urban Growth: An Historical Census*. Lewiston: St. Gourds.

CIA (Central Intelligence Agency). 2005. *World Factbook 2005*. On-line at http://www.cia.gov/cia/publications/factbook/.

City Mayors. 2003. "World Cities." On-line at http://www.citymayors.com/features/urban_areas.html.

De Long, B.J., and A. Shleifer. 1992. Princes and Merchants: European City Growth before the Industrial Revolution. Cambridge, MA: National Bureau of Economic Research and Harvard University (issued in March; revised in December).

de Vries, Jan. 1984. *European Urbanization, 1500–1800*. Cambridge, MA: Harvard University Press.

Kaufmann, Daniel, and Aart Kraay. 2002. "Growth without Governance." *Economia* 3 (1): 169–229. On-line at http://www.worldbank.org/wbi/governance/pubs/growthgov.html.

Kaufmann, Daniel, Frannie Léautier, and Massimo Mastruzzi. 2004. "An Empirical Exploration into Global Determinants of Urban Performance." World Bank Institute Working Papers and Articles (Discussion Paper). Washington, DC: World Bank. On-line at http:/www.worldbank.org/wbi/governance/pdf/govcity.pdf.

Lee, K. S., and A. Anas. 1996. "The Benefits of Alternative Power Tariffs for Nigeria and Indonesia." World Bank Policy Research Working Paper 1606. Washington, DC: World Bank.

Mercer Human Resource Consulting. Various years. "Global Quality of Living Reports." On-line at http://www.mercerhr.com/qol.

UNCHS (United Nations Commission on Human Settlements). 1998. Global Urban Indicators Database. On-line at http://www.unhabitat.org/programmes/guo/guo_indicators.asp.

Russell, Josiah Cox. 1972. *Medieval Regions and Their Cities.* Bloomington: Indiana University Press.

Summers, R., and A. Heston. 1984. "Improved International Comparisons of Real Product and its Composition, 1950–80." *Review of Income and Wealth* 207–61.

World Bank. Various years. World Development Indicators. Washington, DC.

World Economic Forum. Various years. Executive Opinion Survey. Geneva. Prepared for *The Global Competitiveness Report.*

7

Conclusions

Frannie Léautier

In this book, we look at more than 5,000 years of data and writings on cities, their performance with respect to provision of basic services, their governance, and their growth. Cities have always played an important role in shaping global decisions, whether on trade and diplomacy between countries or on culture and governance. Like living organisms, cities are born, they grow, they get sick, and they even die. The more recent speeding up of the process of globalization and its impact on the governance of cities highlights this aspect more sharply and is a subject we revisit in each of the chapters. We have summarized what we have learned at the end of each chapter, and here we pull together the common threads on governance and performance in the context of globalization.

History matters, and city performance is trackable over long periods. Data and evidence from more than 5,000 years indicates that the dynamics of city perform- ance over time can be captured and that this historical assessment sheds light on some of the difficult issues surrounding urban governance (Chapter 5 and 6). Such historical perspectives are particularly important for Africa, which has had high urbanization rates but little increased welfare for residents of cities, limited eco- nomic growth for the countries that have urbanized, scarce foreign direct invest- ment from firms, and well-known challenges for governance (Chapter 4).

Technology and globalization are intensely interlinked. These linkages are manifest when we look at the internationalization of infrastructure (Chapter 2), as well as the impact of technology and globalization on governance (Chapter 6). Insights gained from the international comparison of city infrastructure indicate that the demand for infrastructure is a "derived demand," as infrastructure is not needed for its own sake but for its role in facilitating economic, social, and political activities. Cities cannot advance without infrastructure, but city mayors need to observe a revealed demand for infrastructure to justify its expensive investment. This requires management capability at the city level, especially in light of the increased need to balance local demands with global pressures and to make choices that far surpass the term of any given city mayor.

City management and governance have increased in complexity, pressing the need to develop new institutions that can operate at multiple levels. A city mayor today needs to respond to demand in the long run, balance priorities for its citizens today with those for the next generation, and aggregate diverse preferences, all of which are the key building blocks of good governance (Chapter 3). As democratiza- tion progresses, individual preferences gain priority, pushing for the need to have institutions that can operate at local, regional, national, and multinational levels. Such institutions need to provide means for reaching consensus, as the process of globalization influences many individuals and groups differently. The complexity of managing cities of today is the main reason we have found evidence of good governance at the local level coexisting with weak governance at the global level (Chapter 3). This effect is especially critical in African cities, most of which are poorly governed and not yet globalized; even those that are more globalized are not well governed (Chapter 4). The skills needed to manage cities in a globalizing world are challenging local governments, which are the traditional owners and developers of infrastructure and which must answer primarily to local citizenry. Better attention to the areas where city managers have control, particularly where they exercise autonomy, can be a powerful instrument to better manage the opportunities of globalization (Chapter 4).

Technological advances influence not only globalization, but also governance. Changes in technology for providing infrastructure, as well as the means for financing it at the international level, have brought down costs, as witnessed by the considerable decline in the costs of transport, communication, and energy production (Chapter 2). This has resulted in a speeding up of globalization, but also in the suite of choices that users now have available to meet their service needs. Advancement in technology is thus responsible for both the speeding up of globalization (Chapter 2) and for influencing the quality of governance at the city level (Chapter 6). Management of infrastructure systems that serve cities has increasingly become internationalized (Chapter 2) and that has sealed the initial beginnings of interdependence between urbanization and globalization (Chapter 3). Both globalization and local accountability matter for city performance (Chapter 3 and 5). Interactions between good governance and globalization, which are enabled by technology (Chapter 6), lead to better performance than local accountability alone or globalization by itself (Chapter 3 and 5). Local accountability is affected by technology through citizens' choices to exit and self-provide their own services (such as water or electricity), with the consequent reduction in the need for them to voice their views to local governments (Chapter 5 and 6). Globalization is affected by technology through the lowering of provision costs in transport and communication (Chapter 2) and the better access to information for decision-making through internet, cell phone, and web-based services (Chapter 6).

Good performance has little to do with city size, but good governance is more often sustained in large cities. Using extensive empirical data collected from various sources and stretching more than 5,000 years, we show that there is evidence of a nonlinear relationship between city size and performance, challenging the view that very large cities are necessarily poorly governed or perform poorly with respect to services provided to their citizens (Chapter 3 and 6). Capital cities, which tend to be larger on average than other cities, are found to serve local interests better (for access to sewerage, water, and electricity) than port cities, which tend to depend more on good governance for the city performance variables that matter for globalization (such as access to cell phones and internet). This result indicates that there are different demands for management skill across cities, with some cities—such as port cities—requiring more complex knowledge of demands from both local and global sources, while others—such as capital cities—require management of diverse local demands. This difference could be because political pressures to perform are higher in capital cities, while economic pressures to perform are higher in port cities. Furthermore, we find that in more globalized countries, cities grow at a slower pace than in less globalized countries, even as there is a general slowdown in urbanization in all regions of the world. Thus, we have evidence that cities unable to tap into global opportunities would have to rely on their regional role—serving their hinterland—and hence need to grow much faster to meet the demands of a regional economy (Chapter 4). This could be an explanation for why we find many megacities in developing countries that are not so globalized.

Interactions between mayors, citizens, and firms can be modeled both theoretically and empirically, and the insights from both approaches help us better understand the types of policies that are critical for good city management. Results from extensive empirical work (Chapter 3), cross-variable comparisons (Chapter 4), case studies (Chapter 2), and a theoretical model (Chapter 5) all show the importance of good city governance in the context of globalization. These results suggest that reforms should focus on improving national governance, which can attract investment and increase economic benefits for the country overall. Such improvements also provide a strong platform for cities to improve their own procedural transparency and public participation—in other words, their own management (Chapter 3). Improving governance at the city level allows cities to better translate global opportunities into local value for their citizens (Chapter 3), and this process is observable in the quality of interaction between the mayor, citizens, and firms locating in a given city (Chapter 5).

Africa has particular patterns of urbanization and globalization, and the lessons from the various chapters point to key areas for attention with respect to city performance in Africa. First, Africa should continue in its process of decentralization, improving the competition between cities and local governments at the country level (but more apparent now at a regional level). Decentralization can yield the benefits of both globalization and urbanization (Chapter 4). Second, the benefits of urbanization in Africa can be tapped only if coastal and larger cities start to play a more global or regional role, rather than a national one (Chapter 3 and 4). Third, city managers in Africa need to be better trained to balance the tension between offering services that can make their cities attractive to foreign investment, while continuing to serve the needs of their growing populations and regional economies (Chapter 3, 4, and 5).

Data weaknesses prevent us from making firmer conclusions, and those weaknesses need to be addressed so that policy recommendations can be more effective. The donor community needs to support city governments and intercity networks and partnerships in their globalization efforts. Such support could be in the form of information outreach to get the best firms interested in locating in the city—by, for example, posting procurement information on the web and establishing an e-window for business start-ups. Support could also help to create incentives and strategies for cities to network with each other and tap into global opportunities.